FAVORITE BRAND NAME

BBQ

AND
OUTDOOR
GRILLING

Publications International Ltd.

Nutritional Analysis: Nutritional information is given for some of the recipes in this publication and was submitted in part by the participating companies and associations. Each analysis is based on the food items in the ingredient list and subrecipe ingredient lists, except ingredients listed as optional. When more than one ingredient choice is listed, the first ingredient was used for analysis. Every effort has been made to check the accuracy of these numbers. However, because numerous variables account for a wide range of values for certain foods, nutritional analyses should be considered approximate.

Microwave Cooking: Microwave ovens vary in the wattage. The microwave cooking times given in this publication are approximate. Use the cooking times as guidelines and check for doneness before adding more time.

Contents

Burgers, Ribs & Kabobs

BUFFALO TURKEY KABOBS

⅔ cup HELLMANN'S® or
    BEST FOODS® Real or
    Light Mayonnaise or Low
    Fat Mayonnaise
    Dressing, divided
1 teaspoon hot pepper sauce
1½ pounds boneless turkey
    breast, cut into 1-inch
    cubes
2 red bell peppers *or* 1 red
    and 1 yellow bell pepper,
    cut into 1-inch squares

2 medium onions, cut into
    wedges
¼ cup (1 ounce) crumbled
    blue cheese
2 tablespoons milk
1 medium stalk celery,
    minced
1 medium carrot, minced

In medium bowl combine ⅓ cup of the mayonnaise and hot pepper sauce. Stir in turkey. Let stand at room temperature 20 minutes. On 6 skewers, alternately thread turkey, peppers and onions. Grill or broil 5 inches from heat, brushing with remaining mayonnaise mixture and turning frequently, 12 to 15 minutes. Meanwhile, in small bowl blend remaining ⅓ cup mayonnaise with the blue cheese and milk. Stir in celery and carrot. Serve with kabobs.   *Makes 6 servings*

Note: For best results, use Real Mayonnaise. If using Light Mayonnaise or Low Fat Mayonnaise Dressing, use sauce the same day.

Buffalo Turkey Kabobs

MEXICALI BURGERS

Guacamole (recipe follows)
1 pound ground chuck
⅓ cup purchased salsa or picante sauce
⅓ cup crushed tortilla chips
3 tablespoons finely chopped cilantro
2 tablespoons finely chopped onion
1 teaspoon ground cumin
4 slices Monterey Jack or Cheddar cheese
4 Kaiser rolls or hamburger buns, split
Lettuce leaves (optional)
Sliced tomatoes (optional)

1. Prepare barbecue grill with rectangular metal or foil drip pan. Bank briquets on either side of drip pan for indirect cooking.

2. Prepare Guacamole.

3. Combine beef, salsa, tortilla chips, cilantro, onion and cumin in medium bowl. Mix lightly but thoroughly. Shape mixture into 4 (½-inch-thick) burgers, each 4 inches in diameter.

4. Place burgers on grid. Grill burgers, on covered grill, over medium coals 8 to 10 minutes for medium or until desired doneness is reached, turning halfway through grilling time.

5. Place 1 slice cheese on each burger to melt during last 1 to 2 minutes of grilling. If desired, place rolls, cut-side down, on grid to toast lightly during last 1 to 2 minutes of grilling. Place burgers between rolls; top burgers with Guacamole. Serve with lettuce and tomatoes, if desired.

Makes 4 servings

Guacamole

1 ripe avocado
1 tablespoon purchased salsa or picante sauce
1 teaspoon fresh lime or lemon juice
¼ teaspoon garlic salt

1. Cut avocado lengthwise in half. Remove pit. Scoop avocado flesh out of shells with large spoon; place in medium bowl. Mash roughly with fork or wooden spoon, leaving avocado slightly chunky.

2. Stir in salsa, lime juice and garlic salt. Let stand at room temperature while grilling burgers. Cover and refrigerate if preparing in advance. Bring to room temperature before serving.

Makes about ½ cup

Mexicali Burger

GRILLED PORK AND POTATOES VESUVIO

1 center-cut boneless pork loin
  roast (1½ pounds), well
  trimmed
4 cloves garlic, divided
½ cup dry white wine
2 tablespoons olive oil
1½ to 2 pounds small red
  potatoes (about 1½ inches
  in diameter), scrubbed
6 metal skewers (12 inches
  long)
6 lemon wedges
  Salt (optional)
  Pepper (optional)
¼ cup chopped fresh Italian or
  curly leaf parsley
1 teaspoon finely grated lemon
  peel

1. Cut pork into 1-inch cubes. Place pork in large resealable plastic food storage bag. Mince 3 cloves garlic; place in small bowl. Add wine and oil; mix well. Pour over pork.

2. Place potatoes in single layer in microwave-safe dish. Pierce each potato with tip of sharp knife. Microwave at HIGH (100% power) 6 to 7 minutes or until almost tender when pierced with fork.

(Or, place potatoes in large saucepan. Cover with cold water. Bring to a boil over high heat. Simmer about 12 minutes or until almost tender when pierced with fork.) Immediately rinse with cold water; drain. Add to pork mixture in bag. Seal bag tightly; turn to coat. Marinate in refrigerator at least 2 hours or up to 8 hours, turning occasionally.

3. Prepare barbecue grill.

4. Meanwhile, drain pork mixture; discard marinade. Alternately thread about 3 pork cubes and 2 potatoes onto each skewer. Place 1 lemon wedge on end of each skewer. Sprinkle salt and pepper over pork and potatoes.

5. Place skewers on grid. Grill skewers, on covered grill, over medium coals 14 to 16 minutes or until pork is juicy and barely pink in center and potatoes are tender, turning halfway through grilling time.

6. Remove skewers from grill. Mince remaining garlic. Place in small bowl. Add parsley and lemon peel; mix well. Sprinkle parsley mixture over pork and potatoes. Squeeze lemon wedges over pork and potatoes.

Makes 6 servings

*Grilled Pork and Potatoes
Vesuvio*

MAPLE–GINGER KABOBS

1¼ to 1½ pounds American leg of lamb, cut into 1½-inch cubes

12 tiny new potatoes (about 1¼ pounds)

8 ounces sugar snap peas (about 2 cups)

1 large red bell pepper, cut into 1½-inch squares

6 (12- to 14-inch) metal skewers

Marinade

⅓ cup balsamic vinegar or red wine vinegar

2 tablespoons corn syrup

2 tablespoons water

1 tablespoon olive oil

1 teaspoon grated fresh ginger root

½ teaspoon dried red pepper flakes

½ teaspoon salt

¼ to ½ teaspoon maple flavoring

For marinade, combine vinegar, corn syrup, water, olive oil, ginger root, red pepper flakes, salt and maple flavoring in small bowl. Place a plastic bag in a shallow dish or medium bowl; add meat cubes and marinade. Close bag and refrigerate for several hours or overnight.

If desired, peel potatoes. Cook potatoes in boiling water for 10 to 15 minutes or just until tender; drain. Remove meat from marinade; reserve marinade. Alternate meat cubes, potatoes, snap peas and bell pepper on skewers. Brush generously with reserved marinade.

Grill directly over moderate coals for 10 to 12 minutes or until lamb is done, turning once and brushing with marinade. Discard remaining marinade.

Makes 6 servings

To broil kabobs: place on broiler pan with rack. Broil 5 inches from heat for 10 to 12 minutes, turning once and brushing with marinade as above.

Nutritional Information Per Serving:
Calories 286, Fat 8 g, Sodium 244 mg, Cholesterol 61 mg

Favorite recipe from **American Lamb Council**

COUNTRY GLAZED RIBS

3 to 4 pounds pork baby back ribs, cut into 3- to 4-rib portions

½ cup FRENCH'S® BOLD'N SPICY® Mustard

½ cup packed brown sugar

½ cup finely chopped onion

¼ cup FRENCH'S® Worcestershire Sauce

¼ cup cider vinegar

1 tablespoon mustard seeds

1 teaspoon ground allspice

Honey Mustard Dip (page 13)

Place ribs in large shallow glass baking pan or resealable plastic food storage bag. To prepare marinade, combine mustard, sugar, onion, Worcestershire, vinegar, mustard seeds and allspice in small bowl; mix well. Pour over ribs, turning to coat all sides. Cover and marinate in refrigerator 1 hour or overnight.

Place ribs on grid, reserving marinade. Grill over medium coals 45 minutes or until ribs are barely pink near bone, turning and basting frequently with marinade.

(Do not baste during last 10 minutes of cooking.) Serve with Honey Mustard Dip. Garnish as desired.

Makes 4 to 6 servings

Honey Mustard Dip

½ **cup FRENCH'S® BOLD'N SPICY® Mustard**
½ **cup honey**

Combine mustard and honey in small bowl; mix well.

Makes 1 cup

Prep Time: 10 minutes
Marinate Time: 1 hour
Cook Time: 45 minutes

Country Glazed Ribs

CHICKEN SHISH-KABOBS

¼ cup **CRISCO® Oil**
¼ cup **wine vinegar**
¼ cup **lemon juice**
1 teaspoon **dried oregano leaves**
1 clove **garlic, minced**
¼ teaspoon **black pepper**
1½ pounds **boneless, skinless chicken breasts, cut into 1- to 1½-inch cubes**
12 **bamboo or metal skewers (10 to 12 inches long)**
2 medium **tomatoes, cut into wedges**
2 medium **onions, cut into wedges**
1 medium **green bell pepper, cut into 1-inch squares**
1 medium **red bell pepper, cut into 1-inch squares**
4 cups **hot cooked brown rice (cooked without salt or fat)**
Salt (optional)

1. Combine Crisco Oil, vinegar, lemon juice, oregano, garlic and black pepper in shallow baking dish or glass bowl. Stir well. Add chicken. Stir to coat. Cover. Marinate in refrigerator 3 hours, turning chicken several times.

2. Soak bamboo skewers in water.

3. Prepare grill or heat broiler.

4. Thread chicken, tomatoes, onions and bell peppers alternately on skewers.

5. Place skewers on grill or broiler pan. Grill or broil 5 minutes. Turn. Grill or broil 5 to 7 minutes or until chicken is no longer pink in center. Serve over hot rice. Season with salt and garnish, if desired.

Makes 6 servings

HAWAIIAN HAM & PINEAPPLE KABOBS

¼ cup **molasses**
¼ cup **prepared mustard**
3 tablespoons **vinegar or lemon juice**
2 tablespoons **Worcestershire sauce**
1 teaspoon **TABASCO® pepper sauce**
1½ pounds **cooked ham, cut into 1½-inch cubes***
1 can (1 pound 13 ounces) **pineapple chunks, drained**

*Ham steak may be used.

Thoroughly combine molasses and mustard. Gradually stir in vinegar and Worcestershire sauce. Add Tabasco sauce; mix well. Add ham cubes; stir to coat. Let stand 1 hour.

Alternate ham and pineapple on skewers; brush with sauce. Place on pre-heated grill or under broiler about 4 inches from heat source.

Grill or broil 20 minutes, turning occasionally and brushing with sauce. Serve with remaining heated sauce.

Makes 6 servings

Chicken Shish-Kabobs

SWISS BURGERS

1 package (about 1¼ pounds)
  PERDUE® fresh lean
  ground turkey, ground
  turkey breast meat or
  ground chicken
½ cup thinly sliced scallions
1 teaspoon Worcestershire
  sauce
4 ounces fresh, white
  mushrooms, thinly sliced
2 teaspoons olive oil
½ teaspoon salt
  Ground pepper to taste
4 to 5 pieces Swiss cheese
  Dijon mustard
4 to 5 Kaiser rolls
6 to 8 tablespoons sour cream

Prepare outdoor grill or preheat broiler. In large bowl, combine ground turkey, scallions and Worcestershire sauce. Shape mixture into 4 or 5 patties.

To grill: When coals are medium-hot, place burgers on hottest area of cooking surface of grill; cook 1 to 2 minutes on each side to brown. Move burgers to edge of grill; cook 4 to 6 minutes longer on each side until thoroughly cooked, juices run clear and burgers spring back to the touch.

To broil: Place burgers on rack in broiling pan 4 inches from heat source. Broil 4 to 6 minutes on each side until burgers are thoroughly cooked and spring back to the touch.

Swiss Burger

While burgers are cooking, toss mushrooms with oil and sprinkle lightly with salt and pepper. Place mushrooms on sheet of heavy-duty aluminum foil. Grill or broil along with burgers during last 1 to 2 minutes of cooking time.

When burgers are cooked through, place a piece of Swiss cheese on each; cook 1 minute longer or just enough to melt cheese. To serve, spread mustard on bottom halves of rolls; cover with a burger and an equal portion of mushrooms. Top each with a generous dollop of sour cream and remaining roll half.   *Makes 4 to 5 servings*

HONEY–MUSTARD BURGERS

3 tablespoons Dijon mustard
2 tablespoons honey
3 teaspoons minced fresh oregano leaves,* divided
1 pound ground beef (80% lean)
¼ cup finely chopped onion
¼ teaspoon black pepper
4 leaf lettuce leaves
4 crusty rolls, split
4 onion slices, separated into rings (optional)

Substitute ¾ teaspoon dried oregano leaves, crushed, for fresh oregano. Combine ¼ teaspoon with mustard and honey; add remaining ½ teaspoon to ground beef mixture.

Prepare grill. Combine mustard, honey and 1 teaspoon oregano in small bowl; set aside. Combine ground beef, 2 tablespoons mustard sauce, remaining 2 teaspoons oregano, chopped onion and pepper in large bowl; mix lightly but thoroughly. Divide beef mixture into 4 equal portions; shape into patties 4 inches in diameter.

Place patties on grid. Grill over medium-hot coals 4 to 6 minutes on each side or to desired doneness. Place 1 lettuce leaf on each bottom roll half; top with a burger. Spoon remaining mustard sauce over burgers; garnish with onion rings, if desired. Add top halves of rolls.
          Makes 4 servings

Favorite recipe from **National Cattlemen's Beef Association**

LIPTON® ONION BURGERS

1 envelope LIPTON® Recipe Secrets® Onion Soup Mix
2 pounds ground beef
½ cup water

In large bowl, combine all ingredients; shape into 8 patties. Grill or broil until done.
          Makes 8 servings

BURGERS CANADIAN

½ cup mayonnaise
⅓ cup A.1.® Steak Sauce
2 tablespoons prepared
   horseradish
1 pound ground beef
2 ounces Cheddar cheese,
   sliced
4 slices Canadian bacon
   (4 ounces)
4 sesame sandwich rolls, split
   and lightly toasted
4 curly lettuce leaves

In small bowl, combine mayonnaise, steak sauce and horseradish. Cover; chill until serving time.

Shape ground beef into 4 patties. Grill burgers over medium heat for 4 minutes on each side or to desired doneness. When almost done, top with cheese; grill until cheese melts. Grill Canadian bacon over medium heat for 1 minute on each side or until heated through. Spread 2 tablespoons sauce on each roll bottom; top with burger, warm Canadian bacon slice, lettuce leaf and roll top. Serve immediately with remaining sauce for dipping.

Makes 4 servings

SEASONED BABY BACK RIBS

1 tablespoon paprika
1½ teaspoons garlic salt
1 teaspoon celery salt
½ teaspoon black pepper
¼ teaspoon ground red pepper
4 pounds pork baby back ribs,
   cut into 3- to 4-rib
   portions, well trimmed
Barbecue Sauce (page 19)
Rib rack (optional)

1. Preheat oven to 350°F.

2. For seasoning rub, combine paprika, garlic salt, celery salt, black pepper and ground red pepper in small bowl. Rub over all surfaces of ribs with fingers.

3. Place ribs in foil-lined shallow roasting pan. Bake 30 minutes.

4. Meanwhile, prepare barbecue grill.

5. While coals are heating, prepare Barbecue Sauce.

6. Transfer ribs to rib rack set on grid. Or, place ribs directly on grid. Grill ribs, on covered grill, over medium coals 10 minutes.

7. Remove ribs from rib rack with tongs; brush half the Barbecue Sauce evenly over both sides of ribs. Return ribs to rib rack. Continue to grill, covered, 10 minutes or until ribs are tender and browned. Serve with reserved sauce. Garnish, if desired.

Makes 6 servings

Seasoned Baby Back Ribs

Barbecue Sauce

½ cup ketchup
⅓ cup packed light brown sugar
1 tablespoon cider vinegar
2 teaspoons Worcestershire sauce
2 teaspoons soy sauce

Combine ketchup, brown sugar, vinegar, Worcestershire sauce and soy sauce in glass measuring cup or small bowl. Reserve half of sauce for serving.

Makes about ⅔ cup

ORIENTAL SHRIMP & STEAK KABOBS

1 envelope LIPTON® Recipe Secrets® Savory Herb with Garlic or Onion Soup Mix
¼ cup soy sauce
¼ cup lemon juice
¼ cup olive or vegetable oil
¼ cup honey
½ pound uncooked medium shrimp, peeled and deveined
½ pound boneless sirloin steak, cut into 1-inch cubes
16 cherry tomatoes
2 cups mushroom caps
1 medium green bell pepper, cut into chunks

In large nonaluminum baking dish, blend savory herb with garlic soup mix, soy sauce, lemon juice, oil and honey; set aside. On skewers, alternately thread shrimp, steak, tomatoes, mushrooms and green pepper. Add prepared skewers to baking dish; turn to coat. Cover and marinate in refrigerator at least 2 hours, turning skewers occasionally. Remove prepared skewers, reserving marinade. Grill or broil, turning and basting frequently with reserved marinade, until shrimp turn pink and steak is done. (Do not brush with marinade during last 5 minutes of cooking.)

Makes about 8 servings

Serving Suggestion: Serve with corn-on-the-cob, a mixed green salad and grilled garlic bread.

Oriental Shrimp & Steak Kabobs

THE OTHER BURGER

1 pound ground pork
   (80% lean)
1 teaspoon black pepper
¼ teaspoon salt
   Hamburger buns (optional)

Prepare grill. Gently mix together ground pork, pepper and salt; shape into 4 burgers, each about ¾-inch thick. Place burgers on grid. Grill, on covered grill, over medium-hot coals 5 minutes on each side or until barely pink in center. Serve on hamburger buns, if desired.   *Makes 4 servings*

Eastern Burger: Add 2 teaspoons soy sauce, 2 tablespoons dry sherry and 1 tablespoon grated ginger root to pork mixture; grill as directed.

Veggie Burger: Add 3 drops hot pepper sauce, 1 grated carrot and 3 tablespoons chopped parsley to pork mixture; grill as directed.

South-of-the-Border Burger: Add ¼ teaspoon *each* ground cumin, dried oregano leaves, seasoned salt and crushed red pepper to pork mixture; grill as directed.

Prep time: 10 minutes
Cooking time: 10 minutes

Favorite recipe from **National Pork Producers Council**

HONEY DIJON BARBECUE RIBETTES

2½ pounds baby back pork
     spareribs, split
 2 cloves garlic, minced
 1 tablespoon vegetable oil
 ⅔ cup chili sauce
 ⅓ cup GREY POUPON® Dijon
     Mustard
 ¼ cup honey
 6 thin lemon slices
 ½ teaspoon liquid hot pepper
     seasoning

Place ribs in large heavy pot; fill pot with water to cover ribs. Over high heat, heat to a boil; reduce heat. Cover; simmer for 30 to 40 minutes or until ribs are tender. Drain.

Meanwhile, in medium saucepan, over low heat, cook garlic in oil until tender. Stir in chili sauce, mustard, honey, lemon slices and hot pepper seasoning. Cook over medium heat until heated through, about 2 to 3 minutes. Brush ribs with prepared sauce. Grill over medium heat for 15 to 20 minutes or until done, turning and brushing often with remaining sauce. Slice into individual pieces to serve; garnish as desired. Serve hot.   *Makes 8 servings*

COUNTRY KIELBASA KABOBS

½ cup GREY POUPON®
    COUNTRY DIJON®
    Mustard
½ cup apricot preserves
⅓ cup minced green onions
1 pound kielbasa, cut into
    1-inch pieces
1 large apple, cored and cut
    into wedges
½ cup frozen pearl onions,
    thawed
6 small red skin potatoes,
    parboiled and cut into
    halves
3 cups shredded red and green
    cabbage, steamed

Soak 6 (10-inch) wooden skewers in water for 30 minutes. In small bowl, blend mustard, preserves and green onions; set aside ¼ cup mixture.

Alternately thread kielbasa, apple, pearl onions and potatoes on skewers. Grill or broil kabobs for 12 to 15 minutes or until done, turning and brushing with remaining mustard mixture. Heat reserved mustard mixture and toss with steamed cabbage. Serve hot with kabobs. Garnish as desired.

Makes 6 servings

BASIC BEEFY BURGERS

1 pound lean ground beef
1 cup CORN CHEX® brand
    cereal, crushed to ⅓ cup
1 egg, slightly beaten
2 tablespoons ketchup
½ teaspoon onion powder
⅛ teaspoon garlic powder

1. Combine beef, cereal, egg, ketchup, onion powder and garlic powder. Shape into 5 patties.

2. Grill 10 to 12 minutes or until no longer pink in center, turning once. Serve on buns with cheese slices, tomato, lettuce, pickles, additional ketchup and mustard, if desired.   *Makes 5 servings*

Cheesy Pizza Burgers: Use 3 tablespoons pizza sauce in place of ketchup. Add ⅔ cup shredded mozzarella cheese and ¼ teaspoon dried oregano leaves to beef mixture. Serve on toasted English muffins topped with additional pizza sauce, if desired.

Tasty Taco Burgers: Use 3 tablespoons taco sauce or salsa in place of ketchup. Add ½ teaspoon chili powder and 2 to 3 dashes ground cumin, if desired, to beef mixture. Serve on buns with sliced Monterey Jack or cheddar cheese, shredded lettuce, chopped tomato and additional taco sauce, if desired.

Country Kielbasa Kabobs

Ranch Burger

RANCH BURGERS

1¼ **pounds lean ground beef**
¾ **cup prepared HIDDEN
    VALLEY RANCH®
    Original Ranch® Salad
    Dressing**
¾ **cup dry bread crumbs**
¼ **cup minced onions**
1 **teaspoon salt**
¼ **teaspoon black pepper
    Sesame seed buns
    Lettuce, tomato slices and
    red onion slices (optional)
    Additional Original Ranch®
    Salad Dressing**

In large bowl, combine beef, salad dressing, bread crumbs, onions, salt and pepper. Shape into 6 patties. Grill over medium-hot coals 4 to 5 minutes for medium doneness. Place on sesame seed buns with lettuce, tomato and red onion slices, if desired. Serve with a generous amount of additional salad dressing.

Makes 6 servings

24

CHARCOAL BROILED BURGERS CHA CHA CHA

2 pounds lean ground beef
½ cup *each* prepared salsa and finely crushed tortilla chips
2 teaspoons chili powder
½ teaspoon salt
8 hamburger buns, split
2 cups (8 ounces) SARGENTO® Classic Supreme Shredded Cheese For Tacos
¾ cup chopped fresh tomatoes
¾ cup shredded leaf lettuce or chopped pepperoncini (optional)

Prepare grill. Combine ground beef, salsa, tortilla chips, chili powder and salt in large bowl; mix lightly but thoroughly. Shape into 8 (½-inch-thick) patties, about 4 inches in diameter. Place bun tops, cut sides up, in foil pan large enough to hold in one layer. Divide Taco cheese evenly over bun tops. Cover with foil. Place on one edge of grid and place patties in center of grid. Grill patties over medium-hot coals about 5 minutes on each side for medium or to desired doneness. Serve patties on bun bottoms; top with tomatoes and lettuce or pepperoncini, if desired. Cover with bun tops, cheese sides down.

Makes 8 servings

HOT AND SPICY SPARERIBS

1 rack pork spareribs (3 pounds)
2 tablespoons butter or margarine
1 medium onion, finely chopped
2 cloves garlic, minced
1 can (15 ounces) tomato sauce
⅔ cup cider vinegar
⅔ cup firmly packed brown sugar
2 tablespoons chili powder
1 tablespoon prepared mustard
½ teaspoon black pepper

Melt butter in large skillet over low heat. Add onion and garlic; cook and stir until tender. Add all remaining ingredients except ribs. Bring to a boil over high heat; reduce heat to low and simmer 20 minutes, stirring occasionally.

Prepare grill. Place large piece of heavy-duty foil over coals to catch drippings. Baste meaty sides of ribs with sauce. Place ribs on grid, meaty sides down; baste top side. Grill, on covered grill, about 6 inches over low coals 20 minutes; turn ribs and baste. Cook 45 minutes more or until ribs are tender, basting every 10 to 15 minutes with sauce. (Do not baste during last 5 minutes of grilling.)   *Makes 3 servings*

Favorite recipe from **National Pork Producers Council**

Beef, Pork & Lamb

PORK CHOPS WITH GRILLED PINEAPPLE

1 small pineapple, crown,
  stem and rind removed
  (optional)
½ cup WISH-BONE® Italian
  Dressing
¼ cup pineapple juice

½ cup firmly packed brown
  sugar
3 tablespoons soy sauce
6 pork chops, about 1 inch
  thick (about 2 pounds)

Cut pineapple into 6 crosswise slices; set aside.

In large, shallow nonaluminium baking dish or plastic bag, combine Italian dressing, pineapple juice, sugar and soy sauce. Add chops; turn to coat. Cover, or close bag, and marinate in refrigerator, turning occasionally, 3 to 24 hours.

Remove chops, reserving marinade. Bring reserved marinade to a boil. Grill or broil chops, basting frequently with reserved marinade, until chops are done. While chops are cooking, grill or broil pineapple slices, brushing with boiled marinade, until golden and heated through. If desired, bring remaining reserved marinade to a boil and serve over chops.

Makes 6 servings

Nutritional Information Per Serving: Calories 327, Fat 12 g, Sodium 958 mg,
Cholesterol 59 mg

Pork Chop With Grilled Pineapple

Southern Barbecue Sandwich

SOUTHERN BARBECUE SANDWICH

1 pound boneless sirloin or flank steak
¾ cup FRENCH'S® Worcestershire Sauce, divided
½ cup ketchup
½ cup light molasses
¼ cup FRENCH'S® CLASSIC YELLOW® Mustard
2 tablespoons REDHOT® Cayenne Pepper Sauce
½ teaspoon hickory salt
4 sandwich buns, split

Place steak in large resealable plastic food storage bag. Pour ½ cup Worcestershire over steak. Seal bag and marinate meat in refrigerator 20 minutes.

To prepare barbecue sauce, combine ketchup, molasses, remaining ¼ cup Worcestershire, mustard, RedHot sauce and hickory salt in medium saucepan. Bring to a boil over high heat. Reduce heat to low. Cook 5 minutes until slightly thickened, stirring occasionally. Set aside.

Place steak on grid, discarding marinade. Grill over hot coals 15 minutes, turning once. Remove steak from grid; let stand 5 minutes. Cut steak diagonally into thin slices. Stir steak into barbecue sauce. Cook until heated through, stirring often. Serve steak and sauce in sandwich buns. Garnish as desired.

Makes 4 servings

Prep Time: 15 minutes
Marinate Time: 20 minutes
Cook Time: 25 minutes

SPICY BLACK BEAN TENDERLOIN

2 **pounds pork tenderloin**
Black Bean Sauce (recipe follows)
8 **bay leaves**
1 **tablespoon** *each* **black pepper, dried basil leaves, garlic powder, dried thyme leaves, dried oregano leaves**
1 **teaspoon** *each* **ground cloves, dry mustard and salt**
½ **teaspoon ground cumin**
¼ **teaspoon ground cinnamon**
Hot cooked pasta (optional)

Prepare Black Bean Sauce. Combine all seasonings in blender or food processor; process until bay leaves are fully ground and mixture is smooth.

Prepare grill. Coat tenderloin on all sides with dry rub seasoning. Sear all sides of pork on grill. Place on roasting rack over medium coals. Grill pork about 35 minutes or to an internal temperature of 150°F. Cover and let stand 10 to 15 minutes. To serve, slice tenderloin and fan on serving plates. Drizzle with Black Bean Sauce. Serve with pasta, if desired. *Makes 8 servings*

Black Bean Sauce: Heat 2 tablespoons olive oil in large stockpot; add 1 finely chopped yellow onion, 1 finely chopped carrot and 2 crushed garlic cloves. Cook and stir until onion is translucent. Add 2 cups dried black beans and stir well; add 2 quarts chicken stock and 1 pound ham hocks. Bring to a boil over high heat; reduce heat to medium-low and simmer, partially covered, 1½ hours. Remove ham hocks; discard. Process sauce in food processor or blender in batches. Season with salt and pepper to taste. Keep warm until serving.

Favorite recipe from **National Pork Producers Council**

PORK ROAST WITH HONEY–MUSTARD GLAZE

Wood chunks or chips for smoking
⅓ cup honey
¼ cup whole-seed or coarse-grind prepared mustard
Grated peel and juice of 1 medium orange
1 teaspoon minced fresh ginger *or* ¼ teaspoon ground ginger
½ teaspoon salt
⅛ teaspoon ground red pepper
Apple juice at room temperature
1 boneless pork loin roast (3½ to 4 pounds)

Soak about 4 wood chunks or several handfuls of wood chips in water; drain. Mix honey, mustard, grated orange peel and juice, ginger, salt and red pepper in small bowl.

Arrange medium-low KINGSFORD® Briquets on each side of a rectangular metal or foil drip pan. Pour in apple juice to fill pan half full. Add soaked wood (all the chunks; part of the chips) to the fire.

Oil hot grid to help prevent sticking. Place pork on grid directly above drip pan. Grill pork, on a covered grill, 20 to 30 minutes per pound until meat thermometer inserted in thickest part registers 155°F. (If your grill has a thermometer, maintain a cooking temperature of about 300°F.) Add a few more briquets to both sides of fire every 45 minutes to 1 hour, or as necessary, to maintain a constant temperature. Add more soaked wood chips every 30 minutes. Brush meat with honey-mustard mixture twice during the last 40 minutes of cooking. Let pork stand 10 minutes before slicing to allow the internal temperature to rise to 160°F. Slice and serve with sauce made from pan drippings (directions follow), if desired.

Makes 6 to 8 servings

To make a sauce from pan drippings: Taste the liquid and drippings left in the drip pan. If the drippings have a mild smoky flavor they will make a nice sauce. (If a strong-flavored wood, such as hickory, or too many wood chips were used, the drippings may be overwhelmingly smoky.) Remove excess fat from drip pan with a bulb baster; discard. Measure liquid and drippings; place in a saucepan. For each cup of liquid, use 1 to 2 tablespoons cider vinegar and 2 teaspoons cornstarch mixed with a little cold water until smooth. Stir vinegar-cornstarch mixture into saucepan. Stirring constantly, bring to a boil over medium heat and boil 1 minute. Makes 6 to 8 servings.

ORIENTAL FLANK STEAK

½ cup WISH-BONE® Italian
   Dressing
2 tablespoons firmly packed
   brown sugar
2 tablespoons soy sauce
½ teaspoon ground ginger
   (optional)
1 (1- to 1½-pound) flank or top
   round steak

In large, shallow nonaluminum
baking dish or plastic bag,
combine all ingredients except
steak. Add steak; turn to coat.

Cover, or close bag, and marinate
in refrigerator, turning
occasionally, 3 to 24 hours.

Remove steak, reserving marinade.
Grill or broil steak, turning once,
until steak is done.

Meanwhile, in small saucepan,
bring reserved marinade to a boil
and continue boiling 1 minute.
Pour over steak.

Makes 6 servings

Also terrific with WISH-BONE®
Robusto Italian or Lite Italian
Dressing.

Nutritional Information Per Serving:
Calories 240, Fat 14 g, Sodium 800 mg,
Cholesterol 50 mg

Oriental Flank Steak

RANCH–STYLE FAJITAS

- 2 pounds flank or skirt steak
- ½ cup vegetable oil
- ⅓ cup lime juice
- 2 packages (1 ounce each) HIDDEN VALLEY RANCH® Milk Recipe Original Ranch® Salad Dressing Mix
- 1 teaspoon ground cumin
- ½ teaspoon black pepper
- 6 flour tortillas
  Lettuce
  Guacamole, prepared HIDDEN VALLEY RANCH® Salad Dressing and picante sauce for toppings

Place steak in large baking dish. In small bowl, whisk together oil, lime juice, salad dressing mix, cumin and pepper. Pour mixture over steak. Cover and refrigerate several hours or overnight.

Remove steak; place marinade in small saucepan. Bring to a boil. Grill steak over medium-hot coals 8 to 10 minutes or to desired doneness, turning once and basting with heated marinade during last 5 minutes of grilling. Remove steak and slice diagonally across grain into thin slices. Heat tortillas following package directions. Divide steak strips among tortillas; roll up to enclose. Serve with lettuce and desired toppings.   *Makes 6 servings*

Ranch-Style Fajitas

STEAK AND POTATO SALAD

Roasted Garlic Marinade/Dressing

¾ **cup CRISCO® Savory Seasonings Roasted Garlic Flavor**
¼ **cup red wine vinegar**
1 **tablespoon dijon-style mustard**
1 **teaspoon salt**
½ **teaspoon freshly ground black pepper**
½ **teaspoon sugar**

Salad

1½ **pounds boneless sirloin steak**
2 **pounds small red potatoes, scrubbed**
8 **ounces fresh green beans**
8 **ounces white mushrooms**
1 **medium red bell pepper, cut into small strips**
1 **medium sweet onion, thinly sliced**
1 **cup cherry tomatoes, halved**
¼ **cup chopped parsley**

• For Roasted Garlic Marinade/ Dressing, whisk together all marinade/dressing ingredients until well blended.

• Place steak in plastic bag with resealable top and pour in ⅓ of the marinade/dressing. Allow to remain at room temperature for 30 minutes, then chill until ready to cook.

• Place potatoes in large pot, cover with cold water and bring to boil. Cook for about 20 minutes or until fork-tender. Drain, cool, and cut into quarters. Toss with half of the remaining marinade/dressing.

• Steam green beans for approximately 7 minutes or until crisp-tender. Refresh in ice water and drain.

• Rinse, dry and thinly slice mushrooms. Toss with 2 tablespoons of marinade/dressing to coat.

• Remove steak from marinade and discard marinade from plastic bag. Grill over preheated grill or under preheated broiler to medium doneness. Allow to rest 5 minutes. Cut across grain into thin strips.

• Toss together steak, potatoes, beans, mushrooms, bell pepper and onion. Garnish with tomato halves and parsley.

Makes 6 to 8 servings

GRILLED PORK AND VEGETABLES

⅔ cup soy sauce
2 tablespoons minced fresh ginger
2 tablespoons country-style mustard
2 garlic cloves, crushed
2 teaspoons TABASCO® pepper sauce
2 pork tenderloins, about 1½ pounds
3 medium tomatoes
2 medium zucchini
2 large red onions

In medium bowl, combine soy sauce, ginger, mustard, garlic and hot pepper sauce. Set aside one half of mixture. Add pork tenderloins to bowl. Cover and marinate mixture at least 2 hours or overnight, turning occasionally.

Cut each tomato in half. Cut each zucchini diagonally into ¼-inch-thick slices. Cut onions into ¼-inch-thick slices. Place vegetables in remaining marinade; carefully toss to mix well.

Preheat grill to medium, placing rack 5 to 6 inches above coals. Place pork tenderloins on rack; grill 20 minutes, turning occasionally and brushing with marinade occasionally. (Do not brush with marinade during last 5 minutes of grilling.) Drain tomatoes, zucchini and red onions; reserve marinade. Place vegetables on rack; grill 4 minutes, turning once and brushing occasionally with reserved marinade.
Makes 6 servings

Note: It is important to keep marinade used for pork tenderloin separate from that used for vegetables.

Nutritional Information Per Serving:
Calories 202, Fat 7 g, Sodium 1008 mg, Cholesterol 72 mg

GARLIC–PEPPER STEAK

1¼ teaspoons LAWRY'S® Garlic Powder with Parsley
1¼ teaspoons LAWRY'S® Seasoned Pepper
½ teaspoon LAWRY'S® Seasoned Salt
1 pound sirloin steak

Combine Garlic Powder with Parsley, Seasoned Pepper and Seasoned Salt. Press seasoning mixture into both sides of steak with back of spoon. Let stand 30 minutes. Heat grill for medium coals or heat broiler. Grill or broil, 4 to 5 inches from heat source, 8 to 12 minutes or to desired doneness. *Makes 4 servings*

Presentation: Serve with rice pilaf and a crisp green salad.

Grilled Club Sandwiches

GRILLED CLUB SANDWICHES

1 **long thin loaf (18 inches) French bread**
½ **cup mayonnaise**
¼ **cup FRENCH'S® BOLD 'N SPICY® Mustard**
2 **tablespoons finely chopped red onion**
2 **tablespoons horseradish**
½ **pound sliced smoked boiled ham**
½ **pound sliced honey-baked deli turkey**
1 **large ripe tomato, sliced**
8 **ounces Brie cheese, thinly sliced**
1 **bunch watercress, washed and drained**

Cut bread in half lengthwise. Combine mayonnaise, mustard, onion and horseradish in small bowl; mix well. Spread mixture on both halves of bread. Layer ham, turkey, tomato, cheese and watercress on bottom half of bread. Cover with top half; press down firmly. Cut loaf crosswise into 1½-inch pieces. Thread two mini sandwiches through crusts onto metal skewer. Repeat with remaining sandwiches.

Place sandwiches on well-oiled grid. Grill over medium-low coals about 5 minutes or until cheese is melted and bread is toasted, turning once. Serve warm.

Makes 6 servings

Prep Time: 15 minutes
Cook Time: 5 minutes

BRATS 'N' BEER

1 can or bottle (12 ounces)
   beer (not dark) or
   nonalcoholic beer
4 fresh bratwurst (about
   1 pound)
1 large sweet or Spanish onion,
   (about ½ pound), thinly
   sliced and separated into
   rings
1 tablespoon olive or vegetable
   oil
¼ teaspoon salt
¼ teaspoon pepper
4 hot dog rolls, preferably
   bakery-style or onion, split
   Coarse-grain or sweet-hot
   mustard (optional)
   Drained sauerkraut
   (optional)

1. Prepare barbecue grill for direct cooking.

2. Pour beer into heavy medium saucepan with ovenproof handle. (If not ovenproof, wrap heavy-duty foil around handle.) Set saucepan on one side of grid.

3. Pierce each bratwurst in several places with tip of sharp knife. Carefully add bratwurst to beer; simmer, on uncovered grill, over medium coals 15 minutes, turning once.*

4. Meanwhile, place onion rings on 18×14-inch sheet of heavy-duty foil. Drizzle with oil; sprinkle with salt and pepper. Wrap in foil; place on grid next to saucepan. Grill onions, on uncovered grill, 10 to 15 minutes or until onions are tender.

5. Transfer bratwurst with tongs to grid; remove saucepan using heavy-duty mitt. Discard beer. Grill bratwurst, on covered grill, 9 to 10 minutes or until browned and cooked through, turning halfway through grilling time. If desired, place rolls, cut-side down, on grid to toast lightly during last 1 to 2 minutes of grilling.

6. Place bratwurst in rolls. Open foil packet carefully. Top each bratwurst with onions. Serve with mustard and sauerkraut, if desired.

Makes 4 servings

If desired, bratwurst may be simmered on rangetop. Pour beer into medium saucepan. Bring to a boil over medium-high heat. Carefully add bratwurst to beer. Reduce heat to low and simmer, uncovered, 15 minutes, turning once.

Brat 'n' Beer

Peppered Beef Rib Roast

PEPPERED BEEF RIB ROAST

1 tablespoon plus
    1½ teaspoons black
    peppercorns
2 cloves garlic, minced
1 boneless beef rib roast
    (2½ to 3 pounds), well
    trimmed
¼ cup Dijon-style mustard
¾ cup sour cream
2 tablespoons prepared
    horseradish
1 tablespoon balsamic vinegar
½ teaspoon sugar

1. Prepare barbecue grill with rectangular metal or foil drip pan. Bank briquets on either side of drip pan for indirect cooking.

2. Meanwhile, to crack peppercorns, place peppercorns in heavy, small resealable plastic food storage bag. Squeeze out excess air; seal bag tightly. Pound peppercorns using flat side of meat mallet or rolling pin until cracked. Set aside.

3. Pat roast dry with paper towels. Combine garlic and mustard in small bowl; spread with spatula over top and sides of roast. Sprinkle pepper over mustard mixture.

4. Insert meat thermometer into center of thickest part of roast. Place roast, pepper-side up, on grid directly over drip pan. Grill roast, on covered grill, over medium coals 1 hour to 1 hour 10 minutes or until thermometer registers 150°F for medium-rare or until desired doneness is reached, adding 4 to 9 briquets to each side of the fire after 45 minutes to maintain medium coals.

5. Meanwhile, combine sour cream, horseradish, vinegar and sugar in small bowl; mix well. Cover; refrigerate until serving.

6. Transfer roast to carving board; tent with foil. Let stand 5 to 10 minutes before carving. Serve with horseradish sauce.

Makes 6 to 8 servings

CHILI DOGS

4 to 6 frankfurters
4 to 6 frankfurter buns
1 can (15 ounces) chili without beans
3 tablespoons REDHOT® Cayenne Pepper Sauce
2 teaspoons ground cumin
2 teaspoons chili powder FRENCH'S® French Fried Onions

Place frankfurters and buns on grid. Grill over medium coals 5 minutes or until frankfurters are browned and buns are toasted, turning once.

Combine chili, RedHot sauce, cumin and chili powder in medium saucepan. Bring to a boil over high heat. Reduce heat to low. Cook 3 minutes, stirring often. To serve, place frankfurters into buns. Spoon chili over frankfurters. Top with French Fried Onions.

Makes 4 to 6 servings

Prep Time: 5 minutes
Cook Time: 15 minutes

Tip: Chili topping is also great on hamburgers.

GRILLED HAM STEAKS WITH APRICOT GLAZE

1 pound boneless fully cooked ham, cut into 4 (½-inch-thick) slices
¼ cup apricot jam
2 teaspoons Dijon mustard
2 teaspoons cider vinegar

Prepare grill. Combine jam, mustard and vinegar in small bowl; blend well. Grill ham slices over hot coals 8 to 10 minutes or until lightly browned, brushing with apricot sauce occasionally and turning once. Serve immediately.

Makes 4 servings

Prep time: 15 minutes
Cooking time: 8 to 10 minutes

Favorite recipe from **National Pork Producers Council**

THAI BEEF SALAD

Dressing
- 1 cup prepared olive oil vinaigrette salad dressing
- 1/3 cup REDHOT® Cayenne Pepper Sauce
- 3 tablespoons chopped peeled fresh ginger
- 3 tablespoons sugar
- 3 cloves garlic, chopped
- 2 teaspoons FRENCH'S® Worcestershire Sauce
- 1 cup packed fresh mint or basil leaves, coarsely chopped

Salad
- 1 flank steak (about 1½ pounds)
- 6 cups washed and torn mixed salad greens
- 1 cup sliced peeled cucumber
- 1/3 cup chopped peanuts

Place Dressing ingredients in blender or food processor. Cover and process until smooth. Reserve 1 cup Dressing. Place steak in large resealable plastic food storage bag. Pour remaining Dressing over steak. Seal bag and marinate in refrigerator 30 minutes.

Place steak on grid, reserving marinade. Grill over hot coals about 15 minutes for medium-rare, basting frequently with marinade. Let steak stand 5 minutes. To serve, slice steak diagonally and arrange on top of salad greens and cucumber. Sprinkle with nuts and drizzle with reserved Dressing. Serve warm. Garnish as desired.
Makes 6 servings

Prep Time: 20 minutes
Marinate Time: 30 minutes
Cook Time: 15 minutes

LAMB SIRLOIN WITH HONEY MUSTARD SAUCE

- 1 pound American lamb sirloin steaks, cut ¾ inch thick
  Honey Mustard Sauce (page 41)
- ¼ teaspoon salt
- ¼ teaspoon black pepper

Prepare Honey Mustard Sauce; cover and refrigerate until serving time. Sprinkle lamb steaks with salt and black pepper. Grill or broil 4 inches from heat source for 3 to 5 minutes. Turn and continue cooking 3 to 5 minutes or until desired doneness. Serve with sauce. *Makes 4 servings*

Preparation Time: 15 minutes
Cooking Time: 10 minutes

Honey Mustard Sauce

1 slice firm-textured whole wheat bread (1 ounce), torn into small pieces
¼ cup plain lowfat yogurt
2 tablespoons brown stone-ground mustard
1 tablespoon honey
1 teaspoon snipped parsley
1 teaspoon prepared horseradish
1 to 2 tablespoons water

Combine torn bread and yogurt in medium bowl. Stir until mixture is fairly smooth. Stir in mustard, honey, parsley and horseradish; mix well. Stir in 1 to 2 tablespoons water as necessary to reach desired consistency.

Nutritional Information Per Serving:
Calories 224, Fat 9 g, Sodium 215 mg, Cholesterol 79 mg

Favorite recipe from **American Lamb Council**

Lamb Sirloin with Honey Mustard Sauce

TOURNEDOS WITH MUSHROOM WINE SAUCE DIJON

¼ cup chopped shallots
2 tablespoons
     FLEISCHMANN'S®
     Margarine
1 cup small mushrooms, halved
     (about 4 ounces)
¼ cup GREY POUPON® Dijon
     Mustard, divided
2 tablespoons A.1.® Steak
     Sauce
2 tablespoons Burgundy wine
1 tablespoon chopped parsley
4 slices bacon
4 (4-ounce) beef tenderloin
     steaks (tournedos), about
     1 inch thick
¼ teaspoon coarsely ground
     black pepper

In small saucepan, over medium heat, saute shallots in margarine until tender. Add mushrooms; saute 1 minute. Stir in 2 tablespoons mustard, steak sauce, wine and parsley; heat to a boil. Reduce heat and simmer for 5 minutes; keep warm.

Wrap bacon slice around edge of each steak; secure with toothpicks. Coat steaks with remaining mustard; sprinkle with pepper. Grill steaks over medium heat for 10 to 12 minutes or to desired doneness, turning occasionally. Remove toothpicks; serve steaks topped with warm mushroom sauce.   *Makes 4 servings*

BEEF TENDERLOIN WITH DIJON– CREAM SAUCE

2 tablespoons olive oil
3 tablespoons balsamic vinegar
1 beef tenderloin roast (about
     1½ to 2 pounds)
  Salt
1 tablespoon plus
     1½ teaspoons white
     peppercorns
1 tablespoon plus
     1½ teaspoons black
     peppercorns
3 tablespoons mustard seeds
  Dijon-Cream Sauce (page 43)

Combine oil and vinegar in a cup; rub onto beef. Season generously with salt. Let stand 15 minutes. Meanwhile, coarsely crush peppercorns and mustard seeds in blender or food processor or by hand with mortar and pestle. Roll beef in crushed mixture, pressing into surface to coat.

Oil hot grid to help prevent sticking. Grill beef, on a covered grill, over medium KINGSFORD® Briquets, 16 to 24 minutes (depending on size and thickness of beef) until meat thermometer inserted in center almost registers 150°F for medium-rare, turning halfway through cooking. (Cook until 160°F for medium or 170°F for well-done; add another 5 minutes for every 10°F.) Let stand 5 to 10 minutes before slicing. Slice and serve with a few spoonfuls of Dijon-Cream Sauce.
     Makes 6 servings

Beef Tenderloin with Dijon-Cream Sauce

Dijon-Cream Sauce

- 1 can (14½ ounces) beef broth
- 1 cup whipping cream
- 2 tablespoons butter, softened
- 1½ to 2 tablespoons Dijon mustard
- 1 to 1½ tablespoons balsamic vinegar*
- Coarsely crushed black peppercorns and mustard seeds for garnish

You may substitute 2 teaspoons red wine vinegar plus 1 teaspoon sugar for the balsamic vinegar.

Bring beef broth and whipping cream to a boil in a saucepan. Boil gently until reduced to about 1 cup (sauce will be thick enough to coat a spoon). Remove from heat; stir in butter, a little at a time, until butter is melted. Stir in mustard and vinegar, adjusting amounts to taste. Sprinkle with peppercorns and mustard seeds.

Makes about 1 cup

ROSEMARY–CRUSTED LEG OF LAMB

¼ cup Dijon-style mustard
2 large cloves garlic, minced
1 boneless butterflied leg of lamb (sirloin half, about 2½ pounds), well trimmed
3 tablespoons chopped fresh rosemary leaves *or*
1 tablespoon dried rosemary leaves, crushed
Fresh rosemary sprigs (optional)
Mint jelly (optional)

1. Prepare barbecue grill.

2. Combine mustard and garlic in small bowl; spread half of mixture with fingers or spatula onto one side of lamb. Sprinkle with half of chopped rosemary; pat into mustard mixture. Turn lamb over; repeat with remaining mustard mixture and rosemary.

3. Insert meat thermometer into center of thickest part of lamb.

4. Place lamb on grid. Grill lamb, on covered grill, over medium coals 35 to 40 minutes or until thermometer registers 160°F for

Rosemary-Crusted Leg of Lamb

medium or until desired doneness is reached, turning every 10 minutes.

5. Meanwhile, soak rosemary sprigs in water. Place rosemary sprigs directly on coals during last 10 minutes of grilling.

6. Transfer lamb to carving board; tent with foil. Let stand 10 minutes before carving into thin slices. Serve with mint jelly.

Makes 8 servings

PORK SATAY WITH SPICY PEANUT SAUCE

1 pork tenderloin (about 1 pound), trimmed
1 recipe Tangy Marinade (recipe follows)
1 recipe Spicy Peanut Sauce (recipe follows)
Small bamboo skewers, soaked in water for 1 hour or more

• **Slice** tenderloin across grain into ½ inch slices. **Cut** slices into fourths. **Thread** 5 or 6 pieces onto each skewer. **Place** in shallow glass dish.

• **Pour** Tangy Marinade over skewers. **Cover** with plastic wrap and marinate for 1 to 4 hours in refrigerator.

• **Remove** skewers from dish and **discard** marinade. **Grill** skewers over preheated grill for 6 to 8 minutes or until pork is no longer pink in center, turning once.

• **Serve** hot with Spicy Peanut Sauce for dipping.

Makes 6 to 8 servings

Tangy Marinade

½ cup soy sauce
¼ cup fresh lime juice
3 tablespoons chopped cilantro
2 tablespoons CRISCO® Savory Seasonings Roasted Garlic Flavor
2 tablespoons firmly packed dark brown sugar
¼ teaspoon cayenne pepper

• **Whisk** together all ingredients until well blended.

Spicy Peanut Sauce

¾ cup coconut milk (canned or fresh)
½ cup chicken broth
½ cup creamy peanut butter
¼ cup fresh lime juice
2 tablespoons CRISCO® Savory Seasonings Hot & Spicy Flavor
2 tablespoons firmly packed dark brown sugar
2 tablespoons soy sauce
1 teaspoon minced gingerroot

• **Place** all ingredients in small heavy saucepan. **Bring** to a boil over medium heat, stirring constantly. **Reduce** heat to simmer and **cook** for 10 minutes, while stirring.

• **Serve** hot. (Recipe may be made ahead and reheated in the microwave.)

SUMMER VEGETABLES & FISH BUNDLES

4 fish fillets (about 1 pound)
1 pound thinly sliced
    vegetables*
½ cup water

1 envelope LIPTON® Recipe
    Secrets® Savory Herb
    with Garlic or Golden
    Onion Soup Mix

Use any combination of the following, thinly sliced: mushrooms, zucchini, yellow squash or tomatoes.

On two 18×18-inch pieces heavy-duty aluminum foil, divide fish equally; top with vegetables. Blend water with savory herb with garlic soup mix. Evenly pour over fish. Wrap foil loosely around fillets and vegetables, sealing edges airtight with double fold. Grill or broil pouches, seam sides up, 15 minutes or until fish flakes easily with fork. Serve, if desired, over hot cooked rice.

Makes about 4 servings

*Summer Vegetables &
Fish Bundle*

TURKEY BURRITOS

1 tablespoon ground cumin
1 tablespoon chili powder
1½ teaspoons salt
1½ to 2 pounds turkey
    tenderloin, cut into
    ½-inch cubes
    Avocado-Corn Salsa (recipe
    follows, optional)
    Lime wedges
    Flour tortillas
    Sour cream (optional)
    Tomato slices for garnish

Combine cumin, chili powder and salt in cup. Place turkey cubes in a shallow glass dish or large heavy plastic bag; pour dry rub over turkey and coat turkey thoroughly. Let turkey stand while preparing Avocado-Corn Salsa. Thread turkey onto metal or bamboo skewers. (Soak bamboo skewers in water at least 20 minutes before using to prevent them from burning.)

Oil hot grid to help prevent sticking. Grill turkey, on a covered grill, over medium KINGSFORD® Briquets, about 6 minutes or until turkey is no longer pink in center, turning once. Remove skewers from grill; squeeze lime wedges over skewers. Warm flour tortillas in microwave oven, or brush each tortilla very lightly with water and grill 10 to 15 seconds per side. Top with Avocado-Corn Salsa and sour cream, if desired. Garnish with tomato slices.

Makes 6 servings

Avocado-Corn Salsa

2 small to medium-size ripe
    avocados, finely chopped
1 cup cooked fresh corn or
    thawed frozen corn
2 medium tomatoes, seeded
    and finely chopped
2 to 3 tablespoons chopped
    fresh cilantro
2 to 3 tablespoons lime juice
½ to 1 teaspoon minced hot
    green chili pepper
½ teaspoon salt

Gently stir together all ingredients in medium bowl; adjust flavors to taste. Cover and refrigerate until ready to serve.

Makes about 1½ cups

Tip: This recipe is great for casual get-togethers. Just prepare the fixings and let the guests make their own burritos.

Turkey Burritos

Grilled Swordfish with Pineapple Salsa

GRILLED SWORDFISH WITH PINEAPPLE SALSA

Pineapple Salsa (recipe follows)
1 **tablespoon lime juice**
2 **cloves garlic, minced**
4 **swordfish steaks (about 5 ounces each)**
½ **teaspoon chili powder or coarsely ground black pepper**

Spray cold grid with nonstick cooking spray. Adjust grid 4 to 6 inches above coals. Prepare grill. Prepare Pineapple Salsa; set aside. Combine juice and garlic on plate. Dip swordfish in juice; sprinkle with chili powder. Place fish on grid. Grill, on covered grill, over medium-hot coals 2 to 3 minutes. Turn over; grill 1 to 2 minutes more or until just opaque in center and still very moist. Top each serving with about 3 tablespoons Pineapple Salsa.
Makes 4 servings

Pineapple Salsa
½ **cup finely chopped fresh pineapple**
¼ **cup finely chopped red bell pepper**
1 **green onion, thinly sliced**
2 **tablespoons lime juice**
½ **jalapeño pepper, seeded and minced**
1 **tablespoon chopped fresh cilantro or basil**

Combine ingredients in small glass bowl. Serve at room temperature.
Makes 4 servings

50

CITRUS GRILLED CHICKEN

1 tablespoon Lemon Butter
    Flavor CRISCO® Savory
    Seasonings
¼ cup orange juice
¼ cup lime juice
1 teaspoon Dijon mustard
1 tablespoon honey
2 tablespoons soy sauce
1 teaspoon salt
¼ teaspoon pepper
2 tablespoons chopped parsley
    (or 1 tablespoon dried)
4 boneless, skinless chicken
    breasts

Combine all ingredients except chicken breasts in glass or stainless steel mixing bowl. Whisk until smooth.

Add chicken breasts to marinade. Refrigerate for 2 hours, or overnight, tightly covered.

Remove chicken from marinade. Discard marinade. Heat grill or oven broiler. Grill or broil chicken breasts 7 minutes on each side, or until juices are clear.

Makes 4 servings

FAMILY BARBECUED CHICKEN

5 pounds chicken pieces
1 cup vegetable oil
⅓ cup tarragon vinegar
¼ cup sugar
¼ cup ketchup
1 tablespoon Worcestershire
    sauce
1½ teaspoons dry mustard
1 teaspoon LAWRY'S® Red
    Pepper Seasoned Salt
1 teaspoon LAWRY'S® Garlic
    Powder with Parsley

Place chicken in 12×8×2-inch glass ovenproof dish. In medium bowl, combine remaining ingredients; blend well and pour over chicken. Cover dish and marinate in refrigerator 6 hours or overnight. Bake, covered, in 350°F oven 25 to 30 minutes. Remove chicken, reserving marinade. Heat grill for hot coals. Grill, 4 to 5 inches from heat, about 10 minutes or until no longer pink in center, turning and basting with reserved marinade.

Makes 6 to 8 servings

Presentation: Serve with baked beans and a fresh vegetable salad.

MICROWAVE-BARBECUE DRUMSTICKS

1 package (about 2½ pounds) PERDUE® Oven Stuffer® Roaster Drumsticks (6 drumsticks)
Basting Sauces (3 recipes follow)

Prepare barbecue grill for cooking. Rinse drumsticks and pat dry. Place drumsticks, spoke fashion, on a microwave-safe bacon/roast rack, with the meatiest portions toward outside edges of utensil. Cover loosely with plastic wrap. Microwave at HIGH (100% power) 2 minutes; turn and cook 2 minutes longer at HIGH. Then reduce to MEDIUM–HIGH (70% power). Cook 9 minutes, turn drumsticks over and microwave 9 minutes longer at MEDIUM–HIGH.

Arrange drumsticks on barbecue grill about 8 inches above medium-hot coals. Grill 15 to 20 minutes, turning drumsticks frequently and brushing with Basting Sauce of choice. Remove from grill; cover. Let stand 5 minutes and test for doneness (juice should run clear when drumstick is pierced with a fork). *Makes 2 to 4 servings*

Note: Other oven stuffer parts may be microwave-grilled following the above directions. For broiler-sized chicken parts, microwave 10 to 12 minutes at HIGH, then grill 15 minutes.

Basting Sauces
Honey Lemon Sauce

½ cup honey
¼ cup butter or margarine, melted
2 tablespoons fresh lemon juice
2 teaspoons grated lemon peel
½ to 1 teaspoon dried dillweed

In a small bowl, combine all ingredients. Brush on chicken during grilling.

Ranch Sauce

½ cup cider vinegar
⅓ cup vegetable oil
1 clove garlic, minced
1½ teaspoons Worcestershire sauce
1½ teaspoons steak sauce
1 teaspoon salt
1 teaspoon paprika
¼ teaspoon instant minced onion
¼ teaspoon dry mustard
6 to 8 drops hot pepper sauce

In a pint jar, combine all ingredients; cover and shake to blend. Brush on chicken during grilling.

Sweet and Sour Sauce

⅓ cup apricot preserves
1 tablespoon plus 1½ teaspoons cider vinegar
1 tablespoon butter or margarine, melted
¼ teaspoon ground ginger
¼ teaspoon salt

In a small bowl, combine all ingredients. Brush on chicken during grilling.

Grilled Chicken Skewers

GRILLED CHICKEN SKEWERS

2 **boneless, skinless chicken breast halves (about ½ pound), cut into thin strips**
½ **pound bacon slices**
⅓ **cup lemon juice**
⅓ **cup honey**
1½ **teaspoons LAWRY'S® Lemon Pepper Seasoning**
½ **teaspoon LAWRY'S® Seasoned Salt**

Thread chicken strips and bacon slices onto wooden skewers. In shallow glass dish, combine remaining ingredients. Add prepared skewers; cover dish and marinate in refrigerator 1 hour or overnight. Heat grill for medium coals or heat broiler. Remove skewers, reserving marinade. Grill or broil skewers, 4 to 5 inches from heat source, 10 to 15 minutes or until chicken is no longer pink in center and bacon is crisp, basting with reserved marinade.

Makes 2 servings

Hint: Soak wooden skewers in water before adding chicken and bacon to prevent skewers from burning.

HEALTHY GRILLED CHICKEN SALAD

½ cup A.1.® Steak Sauce
½ cup prepared Italian salad
   dressing
 1 teaspoon dried basil leaves
 1 pound boneless chicken
   breast halves
 6 cups mixed salad greens
¼ pound snow peas, blanched
   and halved
 1 cup sliced mushrooms
 1 medium red bell pepper,
   thinly sliced
   Grated Parmesan cheese
   (optional)

In small bowl, combine steak sauce, dressing and basil. Place chicken in glass dish; coat with ¼ cup steak sauce mixture. Cover; chill 1 hour, turning occasionally.

Arrange salad greens, peas, mushrooms and pepper slices on 6 individual salad plates; set aside.

In small saucepan, over medium heat, heat remaining steak sauce mixture; keep dressing warm.

Remove chicken from marinade; discard marinade. Grill over medium heat for 8 to 10 minutes or until no longer pink in center, turning occasionally. Thinly slice chicken; arrange over salad greens and drizzle warm dressing over prepared salads. Serve immediately; sprinkle with Parmesan cheese if desired.   *Makes 6 servings*

Healthy Grilled Chicken Salad

GRILLED PINEAPPLE RICE SALAD WITH TUNA

Rice Salad

- 3 cups cooked **RICELAND®** Extra Long Grain Rice
- 2 teaspoons grated orange zest
- ½ cup orange juice
- 3 tablespoons fresh lime juice
- 1 garlic clove, minced
- 1 cup cooked black beans
- 1 cup whole kernel corn
- ½ cup diced red bell pepper
- ¼ cup chopped fresh cilantro
  Lettuce leaves

Grilled Tuna/Pineapple

- 6 tuna steaks, 1 inch thick*
- ½ large pineapple, peeled, cored and quartered
- 2 tablespoons oil
- 3 tablespoons fresh lime juice
- 2 garlic cloves, minced
- 1 teaspoon Italian seasoning
  Fresh ground pepper

Boneless, skinless chicken breasts may be substituted.

In large bowl, combine rice, orange zest, orange juice, lime juice and garlic. Add remaining salad ingredients; toss lightly. Cover and hold at room temperature.

Prepare grill. Rinse tuna; pat dry. Prepare pineapple. Combine remaining ingredients; brush over tuna and pineapple. Grill tuna for approximately 5 minutes per side, basting with marinade. Place pineapple on outer edge of grill, turning and basting until lightly browned.

Chop grilled pineapple and toss into rice salad. Place lettuce leaves on serving plates. Spoon rice mixture on top and place tuna steak on center.

GRILLED SALMON WITH CUCUMBER SAUCE

- ¾ cup **HELLMANN'S®** or **BEST FOODS®** Real or Light Mayonnaise or Low Fat Mayonnaise Dressing
- ¼ cup snipped fresh dill *or* 1 tablespoon dried dill weed
- 1 tablespoon lemon juice
- 6 salmon steaks (4 ounces each), ¾ inch thick
- 1 small cucumber, seeded and chopped
- ½ cup chopped radishes
  Lemon wedges

In medium bowl combine mayonnaise, dill and lemon juice; reserve ½ cup for sauce. Brush fish steaks with remaining mayonnaise mixture. Grill 6 inches from heat, turning and brushing frequently with mayonnaise mixture, 6 to 8 minutes or until fish is firm but moist. Stir cucumber and radishes into reserved mayonnaise mixture. Serve fish with cucumber sauce and lemon wedges.

Makes 6 servings

GRILLED CHICKEN TORTILLAS

3 whole broiler-fryer chicken breasts, halved, boned, skinned
  Juice of 2 limes
3 tablespoons olive oil
1 clove garlic, crushed
½ teaspoon salt
¼ teaspoon bottled hot pepper sauce
12 flour tortillas
3 cups shredded lettuce
2 cups diced tomatoes
1½ cups shredded Monterey Jack cheese
1 jar (10 ounces) chunky salsa

In large, non-metallic container, mix lime juice, olive oil, garlic, salt, and hot pepper sauce. Add chicken; turn to coat with marinade. Marinate in refrigerator at least 1 hour. Stack tortillas; wrap in foil and set aside. Remove chicken from marinade; discard marinade. Place chicken on prepared grill about 8 inches from heat source. Grill, turning frequently, 16 to 20 minutes or until chicken is fork-tender. While chicken is cooking, heat tortillas by placing foil-wrapped package on side of grill; grill until warmed, turning package once or twice. Remove chicken to platter; cut into ¼-inch strips. To assemble, spread ¼ cup lettuce over each tortilla. Top with chicken, tomatoes and cheese. Drizzle with salsa; roll up.

Makes 6 servings

Favorite recipe from **Delmarva Poultry Industry, Inc.**

GRILLED GAME HENS

½ cup K.C. MASTERPIECE® Barbecue Sauce
¼ cup dry sherry
3 tablespoons frozen orange juice concentrate, thawed
4 Cornish game hens (each about 1 to 1½ pounds)

Combine barbecue sauce, sherry and orange juice concentrate in a small saucepan. Bring to a boil. Simmer 10 minutes; cool. Rinse hens; pat dry with paper towels. Brush sauce onto hens. Oil hot grid to help prevent sticking. Grill hens, on a covered grill, over medium-hot KINGSFORD® Briquets, 40 to 50 minutes or until thigh moves easily and juices run clear when pierced with fork, turning once. Baste with sauce during last 10 minutes of grilling. Remove hens from grill; baste with sauce.

Makes 4 to 6 servings

HONEY-MUSTARD ALASKA HALIBUT

¼ **cup Dijon-style mustard***
¼ **cup butter, melted***
2 **tablespoons honey***
2 **teaspoons lemon juice***
6 **(4 to 6 ounces each) Alaska halibut steaks**
  Salt and black pepper
  Vegetables for skewering, such as cherry tomatoes, red onion wedges, red or green bell pepper chunks, zucchini chunks, boiled new potatoes (optional)

* *If desired, double these sauce ingredients and serve extra sauce, warm, as a dipping sauce.*

Whisk together mustard, butter, honey and lemon juice. Season halibut steaks with salt and black pepper. Brush both sides of each halibut steak liberally with mustard mixture. Place on a well-oiled grill or broiling pan 5 to 6 inches from heat source. Grill or broil for 10 minutes per inch of thickness, or until fish flakes easily when tested with a fork. Cut halibut into 1-inch chunks and alternately place on skewers with an assortment of vegetables. Broil or grill as directed above again until vegetables are crisp-tender.

Makes 6 servings

Favorite recipe from **Alaska Seafood Marketing Board**

Honey-Mustard Alaska Halibut

Blackened Sea Bass

BLACKENED SEA BASS

Hardwood charcoal*
2 teaspoons paprika
1 teaspoon garlic salt
1 teaspoon dried thyme leaves,
    crushed
¼ teaspoon ground white
    pepper
¼ teaspoon ground red pepper
¼ teaspoon ground black
    pepper
3 tablespoons butter or
    margarine
4 skinless sea bass or catfish
    fillets (4 to 6 ounces each)
Lemon halves
Fresh dill sprigs for garnish

Hardwood charcoal takes somewhat longer than regular charcoal to become hot, but results in a hotter fire than regular charcoal. A hot fire is necessary to seal in the juices and cook fish quickly. If hardwood charcoal is not available, scatter dry hardwood, or mesquite or hickory chunks over hot coals to create a hot fire.

1. Prepare barbecue grill using hardwood charcoal.

2. Meanwhile, combine paprika, garlic salt, thyme, and white, red and black peppers in small bowl; mix well. Set aside.

3. Melt butter in small saucepan over medium heat. Pour melted butter into pie plate or shallow bowl. Cool slightly.

4. Dip sea bass into melted butter, evenly coating both sides.

5. Sprinkle both sides of sea bass evenly with paprika mixture.

6. Place sea bass on grid. (Fire will flare up when sea bass is placed on grid, but will subside when grill is covered.) Grill sea bass, on covered grill, over hot coals 4 to 6 minutes or until sea bass is blackened and flakes easily when tested with fork, turning halfway through grilling time. Serve with lemon halves. Garnish, if desired.

Makes 4 servings

GRILLED SALMON SALAD

1 pound boneless salmon fillet
6 cups torn mixed greens
6 red-skinned new potatoes, cooked, sliced
1 cup fresh green bean pieces, cooked, chilled
1 cup seedless cucumber slices
2 plum tomatoes, sliced
    Mustard Vinaigrette (recipe follows)

1. Grill salmon over medium-high coals until fish flakes easily with a fork, about 10 minutes.

2. Meanwhile, place greens on individual serving plates. Arrange potatoes, green beans, cucumber and tomatoes over greens. Break cooked salmon into chunks with fork; arrange on salads.

3. Serve with Mustard Vinaigrette.
Makes 4 servings

Variation: Substitute 1 pound boneless, skinless chicken breast halves for salmon. Grill 5 to 7 minutes on each side or until center is no longer pink; slice. Continue as directed.

Mustard Vinaigrette
½ cup olive oil
⅓ cup lemon juice
3 tablespoons PLOCHMAN'S® Mild Yellow or Dijon Mustard
1 tablespoon water
2 teaspoons minced fresh tarragon leaves *or* ¾ teaspoon dried tarragon leaves
½ teaspoon sugar
¼ teaspoon salt

Mix together all ingredients with a wire whisk.

Variation: Substitute 4 teaspoons minced fresh dill weed or 1 teaspoon dried dill weed for tarragon.

Preparation & Cooking Time:
    40 minutes

ROTELLE WITH GRILLED CHICKEN DIJON

¾ cup **GREY POUPON® Dijon Mustard, divided**
1 tablespoon **lemon juice**
1 tablespoon **olive oil**
1 clove **garlic, minced**
½ teaspoon **Italian seasoning**
1 pound **boneless, skinless chicken breasts**
¼ cup **FLEISCHMANN'S® Margarine**
1 cup **COLLEGE INN® Chicken Broth or Lower Sodium Chicken Broth**
1 cup **chopped cooked broccoli**
⅓ cup **coarsely chopped roasted red peppers**
1 pound **tri-color rotelle or spiral-shaped pasta, cooked**
¼ cup **grated Parmesan cheese**

In medium bowl, combine ¼ cup mustard, lemon juice, oil, garlic and Italian seasoning. Add chicken, stirring to coat well. Refrigerate for 1 hour.

Grill or broil chicken over medium heat for 6 minutes on each side or until done. Cool slightly; slice into ½-inch strips and set aside.

In large skillet, over medium heat, melt margarine; blend in remaining mustard and chicken broth. Stir in broccoli and peppers; heat through. In large serving bowl, combine hot cooked pasta, broccoli mixture, chicken and Parmesan cheese; toss to coat well.   *Makes 5 servings*

SHRIMP ON THE BARBIE

1 pound **large raw shrimp, shelled and deveined**
1 *each* **red and yellow bell pepper, seeded and cut into 1-inch chunks**
4 slices **lime (optional)**
½ cup **prepared smoky-flavor barbecue sauce**
2 tablespoons **FRENCH'S® Worcestershire Sauce**
2 tablespoons **REDHOT® Cayenne Pepper Sauce**
1 clove **garlic, minced**

Thread shrimp, peppers and lime, if desired, alternately onto metal skewers. Combine barbecue sauce, Worcestershire, RedHot sauce and garlic in small bowl; mix well. Brush on skewers.

Place skewers on grid, reserving sauce mixture. Grill over hot coals 15 minutes or until shrimp turn pink, turning and basting often with sauce mixture. (Do not baste during last 5 minutes of cooking.) Serve warm.   *Makes 4 servings*

Prep Time: 10 minutes
Cook Time: 15 minutes

Rotelle with Grilled Chicken Dijon

MARINATED CHICKEN WINGS WITH RED HOT HONEY MUSTARD DIPPING SAUCE

12 chicken wings (about
      2½ pounds), split at joint,
      tips discarded
¼ cup soy sauce
3 tablespoons PLOCHMAN'S®
      Mild Yellow or Dijon
      Mustard
2 tablespoons frozen orange
      juice concentrate, thawed
2 tablespoons honey
1 teaspoon grated orange rind
      Red Hot Honey Mustard
      Dipping Sauce (recipe
      follows)

1. Place chicken wings in glass 12×8-inch baking dish. Combine soy sauce, mustard, orange juice, honey and orange rind. Pour over chicken wings; toss to coat. Marinate in refrigerator 2 hours or overnight, stirring occasionally.

2. Drain marinade from chicken, reserving marinade. Arrange chicken wings on greased grid of grill. Grill over medium coals 15 minutes on each side, basting with reserved marinade halfway through cooking time. Discard any unused marinade. Serve with Hot Honey Mustard Dipping Sauce.
      Makes 8 appetizer servings

Prep & Cook Time: 45 minutes
Marinating Time: 2 hours

RED HOT HONEY MUSTARD DIPPING SAUCE

⅓ cup honey
3 tablespoons PLOCHMAN'S®
      Mild Yellow or Dijon
      Mustard
1 to 2 teaspoons hot pepper
      sauce

Mix together all ingredients.

SHANGHAI FISH PACKETS

4 orange roughy or tilefish
      fillets (4 to 6 ounces each)
¼ cup mirin* or Rhine wine
3 tablespoons soy sauce
1 tablespoon sesame oil
1½ teaspoons grated fresh
      gingerroot
¼ teaspoon crushed red pepper
1 package (10 ounces) fresh
      spinach leaves
1 tablespoon vegetable oil
1 clove garlic, minced

Mirin is a Japanese sweet wine available in Japanese markets and the gourmet section of large supermarkets.

1. Prepare barbecue grill.

2. Place orange roughy in single layer in large shallow dish. Combine mirin, soy sauce, sesame oil, ginger and crushed red pepper in small bowl; pour over orange roughy. Cover; marinate in refrigerator while preparing spinach.

3. Wash spinach leaves in cold water; remove and discard stems. Pat leaves dry with paper towels.

4. Heat vegetable oil in large skillet over medium heat. Add garlic; cook and stir 1 minute. Add spinach; cook and stir until wilted, about 3 minutes.

5. Place spinach mixture in center of each of 4 (12-inch) squares of heavy-duty foil. Remove orange roughy from marinade; reserve marinade. Place 1 orange roughy fillet over each mound of spinach. Drizzle reserved marinade evenly over orange roughy. Wrap in foil.

6. Place packets on grid. Grill packets, on covered grill, over medium coals 15 to 18 minutes or until orange roughy flakes easily when tested with fork.

Makes 4 servings

Shanghai Fish Packet

Sizzling Chicken Sandwich

SIZZLING CHICKEN SANDWICHES

4 boneless, skinless chicken
   breast halves (about
   1 pound)
1 package (1.27 ounces)
   LAWRY'S® Spices &
   Seasonings for Fajitas
1 cup chunky salsa
¼ cup water
   Lettuce
4 large sandwich buns
4 slices Monterey Jack cheese
   Red onion slices
   Avocado slices
   Additional chunky salsa

In large resealable plastic bag, place chicken. In small bowl, combine Spices & Seasonings for Fajitas, 1 cup salsa and water; pour over chicken. Marinate in refrigerator 2 hours. Heat grill for medium coals or heat broiler. Remove chicken, reserving marinade. Grill or broil, 4 to 5 inches from heat source, 5 to 7 minutes on each side or until chicken is no longer pink in center, basting frequently with marinade. Place on lettuce-lined sandwich buns. Top with cheese, onion, avocado and salsa.

Makes 4 servings

Hint: Do not baste chicken with marinade during last 5 minutes of cooking.

SOUTHWESTERN MARINATED FISH

6 fish fillets (any firm fish such as halibut, swordfish, tuna, etc.)
1 cup tomato sauce (8-ounce can)
½ cup CRISCO® Savory Seasonings Roasted Garlic Flavor
¼ cup lemon or lime juice
1 to 2 tablespoons chili powder
1 teaspoon salt
Roasted Corn Salsa (page 69)

• Place fish in shallow dish or heavy duty plastic bag with resealable top.

• Whisk together remaining ingredients and pour over fish. Marinate in refrigerator in covered dish or sealed plastic bag for 30 minutes, or up to 2 hours.

• Remove fish from marinade and discard marinade. Grill over preheated grill until lightly browned and cooked through, turning over once. (Note: A fish fillet one inch thick will be done in approximately 10 minutes.)

• Serve with Roasted Corn Salsa.
Makes 5 servings

Variation: Large shrimp, prawns or boneless chicken breasts may be substituted for fish fillets.

APRICOT GLAZED CHICKEN

½ cup WISH-BONE® Italian Dressing
2 teaspoons ground ginger (optional)
1 (2½- to 3-pound) chicken, cut into serving pieces
¼ cup apricot or peach preserves

In large, shallow nonaluminum baking dish or plastic bag, blend Italian dressing and ginger. Add chicken; turn to coat. Cover, or close bag, and marinate in refrigerator, turning occasionally, 3 to 24 hours.

Remove chicken from marinade, reserving ¼ cup marinade. In small saucepan, bring reserved marinade to a boil and continue boiling 1 minute. Remove from heat and stir in preserves until melted; set aside.

Grill or broil chicken until chicken is done, brushing with preserves mixture during last 5 minutes of cooking.   *Makes 4 servings*

Also terrific with WISH-BONE® Robusto Italian Dressing.

Nutritional Information Per Serving:
Calories 545, Fat 32 g, Sodium 731 mg, Cholesterol 182 mg

Sauces & Marinades

OLD–FASHIONED CORN RELISH

⅓ cup cider vinegar
2 tablespoons sugar
1 tablespoon cornstarch
3 tablespoons FRENCH'S®
    CLASSIC YELLOW®
    Mustard
¼ teaspoon seasoned salt
1 package (9 ounces) frozen
    corn, thawed and
    drained

½ cup chopped celery
½ cup chopped red bell
    pepper
¼ cup finely chopped red
    onion
3 tablespoons sweet pickle
    relish

Combine vinegar, sugar and cornstarch in large microwave-safe bowl; mix well. Stir in mustard and salt. Microwave, uncovered, on HIGH 1 to 2 minutes or until thickened, stirring once. Add corn, celery, pepper, onion and pickle relish; toss well to coat evenly. Cover and refrigerate 30 minutes before serving. Serve as a relish on hamburgers or hot dogs, or serve on the side with grilled meats. *Makes about 3 cups*

Prep Time: 10 minutes
Cook Time: 2 minutes
Chill Time: 30 minutes

Top to bottom: Corn & Bean Salsa (page 70), Old-Fashioned Corn Relish

Orange-Cumin Marinade for Chicken

ORANGE–CUMIN MARINADE FOR CHICKEN

¼ cup frozen orange juice
   concentrate
2 tablespoons water
2 teaspoons onion powder
1 teaspoon garlic powder
1 teaspoon ground cumin
¾ teaspoon salt
⅛ teaspoon ground red pepper
1¼ pounds boned and skinned
   chicken breasts (cutlets)

In a shallow glass baking dish, combine orange juice, water, onion and garlic powders, cumin, salt and red pepper. Pierce chicken with fork tines on both sides. Add chicken to marinade; turn to coat both sides. Cover and let stand for 10 to 15 minutes. Pour excess marinade into small saucepan; bring to a boil. Lightly spray chicken with nonstick cooking spray. Place chicken on a rack over hot coals or under a preheated broiler. Grill, brushing frequently with heated marinade, until juices run clear, 4 to 5 minutes on each side.

Makes 4 servings

Nutritional Information Per Serving:
Calories 203, Fat 2 g, Sodium 507 mg,
Cholesterol 82 mg

Favorite recipe from **American Spice Trade Association**

ROASTED CORN SALSA

4 medium ears of corn, shucked
3 tablespoons CRISCO® Savory Seasonings Hot & Spicy Flavor
1 cup chopped onion
1½ cups diced Roma tomatoes
¼ cup chopped cilantro
2 tablespoons fresh lime juice
¾ teaspoon salt

1. **Rub** surface of corn with 1 tablespoon of oil to coat lightly.

2. **Grill** corn over preheated grill or under preheated broiler with corn 4 to 6 inches from heat source for 15 minutes, turning to cook all sides of corn.

3. **Cool** and **cut** corn kernels from cob.

4. **Heat** remaining 2 tablespoons of oil in a skillet. **Sauté** onion for 1 minute. **Add** diced tomatoes and **cook** 1 minute more, stirring.

5. **Add** onion and tomatoes to the corn. **Season** with cilantro, lime juice and salt. **Serve** at room temperature or **cover** and **chill** until ready to serve.

Makes about 4 cups

PLUM BARBECUE SAUCE

6 cups Plum Purée (recipe follows)
1 cup *each* granulated sugar and packed brown sugar
1 tablespoon black pepper
1½ teaspoons salt
¾ teaspoon onion powder
¾ teaspoon celery seed
¾ teaspoon garlic powder
¼ teaspoon cayenne
½ teaspoon ground cumin
½ teaspoon dried oregano leaves
4 teaspoons liquid smoke (optional)

Combine all ingredients in stainless steel or enamel pot; simmer gently, stirring occasionally, about 1 hour.

Makes about 5 cups

Plum Purée

8 pounds fresh California plums (about 48 medium plums)

Cut plums in half; remove pits. Slice plums; place in large heavy saucepan. Cook over medium heat, stirring occasionally, about 45 minutes. (If red plums are used, red skins will impart a rosy color to the puree.) Strain to remove pulp and skins.

Makes about 12 cups

Nutritional Information Per Serving:
Calories 121, Fat 1 g, Cholesterol 0 mg

Favorite recipe from **California Tree Fruit Agreement**

ZESTY GARLIC MARINADE

½ cup Roasted Garlic Flavor
    CRISCO® Savory
    Seasonings
  Juice of 1 lemon (or
    3 tablespoons bottled or
    frozen lemon juice)
1 teaspoon Dijon mustard
½ teaspoon hot pepper sauce
    (or to taste)
1 teaspoon salt
1 tablespoon brown sugar or
    honey
4 to 6 boneless chicken
    breasts, pork chops or
    steak

1. Whisk together all ingredients except chicken with a wire whisk or a fork until well blended.

2. Pour mixture over boneless chicken breasts, pork chops or steak. Let stand at room temperature for 30 minutes. (Note: Marinating meats longer than 30 minutes will require refrigeration of the meat/ marinade mixture.)

3. Broil or grill until done, turning the marinated chicken, chops or steak once.

Makes 4 to 6 servings

CORN & BEAN SALSA

⅓ cup olive oil
3 tablespoons REDHOT®
    Cayenne Pepper Sauce
3 tablespoons red wine vinegar
2 tablespoons minced fresh
    cilantro leaves
1 clove garlic, minced
½ teaspoon chili powder
¼ teaspoon salt
1 package (9 ounces) frozen
    corn, thawed and drained
1 can (16 ounces) black beans,
    drained and rinsed
1 large ripe tomato, chopped
2 green onions, thinly sliced

Whisk together oil, RedHot sauce, vinegar, cilantro, garlic, chili powder and salt in large bowl until blended. Add corn, beans, tomato and onions; toss well to coat evenly. Cover and refrigerate 30 minutes before serving. Serve with grilled steak or hamburgers.

Makes 6 servings
(about 4 cups salsa)

Prep Time: 15 minutes
Chill Time: 30 minutes

ONION WINE SAUCE

4 cups onion wedges
2 cloves garlic, minced
2 tablespoons
   FLEISCHMANN'S®
   Margarine
½ cup A.1.® Steak Sauce
2 tablespoons red cooking
   wine

In large skillet, over medium-high heat, cook and stir onions and garlic in margarine until tender, about 10 minutes. Stir in steak sauce and wine; heat to a boil. Reduce heat; simmer 5 minutes. Serve hot with cooked beef or poultry.   *Makes 2½ cups*

CREAMY HORSERADISH SAUCE

1 (8-ounce) package cream
   cheese, softened
⅓ cup A.1.® Steak Sauce
3 tablespoons prepared
   horseradish, drained
2 tablespoons chopped green
   onion

In medium bowl, blend cream cheese, steak sauce and horseradish; stir in onion. Cover; chill at least 1 hour or up to 2 days. Serve cold or at room temperature with cooked beef, sausage, fish or baked potatoes.
          Makes 1½ cups

Onion Wine Sauce

Easy Honey Mustard Barbecue Sauce

EASY HONEY MUSTARD BARBECUE SAUCE

1 bottle (10.5 ounces) PLOCHMAN'S® Mild Yellow Mustard (about 1 cup)
½ cup barbecue sauce
¼ cup honey
2 tablespoons finely minced onion

Mix all ingredients. Use as a condiment, or brush on chicken, pork chops or seafood.

Makes 2 cups

Preparation Time: 5 minutes

LEMON–GARLIC GRILLING SAUCE

½ cup butter or margarine, melted
¼ cup fresh lemon juice
1 tablespoon Worcestershire sauce
½ teaspoon TABASCO® pepper sauce
1 to 3 cloves garlic, minced
¼ teaspoon black pepper

Combine ingredients in small bowl; mix until well blended. Brush on fish, seafood, poultry or vegetables during grilling or broiling. Heat any remaining sauce to a boil and serve with grilled foods. *Makes ¾ cup*

LONE STAR BARBECUE SAUCE

½ cup butter, melted
¼ cup sugar
¼ teaspoon TABASCO® pepper
   sauce
½ teaspoon dry mustard
1 cup vegetable oil
1 bottle (12 ounces) ketchup
¼ cup Worcestershire sauce
2 cloves garlic, minced
1 large onion, chopped
   Juice from 1 lemon

Combine all ingredients in medium bowl until well blended. Brush both sides of beef or chicken before grilling and frequently during grilling. (Do not baste during last 5 minutes of grilling.)

Makes about 3½ cups

SOUTHWEST SPICY–LIME MARINADE

½ cup CRISCO® Savory
   Seasonings Hot & Spicy
   Flavor
2 tablespoons lime juice
1 to 2 teaspoons Dijon mustard
1 teaspoon sugar
½ teaspoon salt

1. Blend ingredients together with fork or whisk until smooth.

2. Marinate chicken breasts, pork or steak in a resealable plastic bag or shallow dish (for up to 24 hours).

3. Grill or broil, turning once, until thoroughly cooked.

Makes about ⅔ cup marinade

RED WINE MARINADE

⅓ cup red wine vinegar
2 tablespoons vegetable oil
1 tablespoon Dijon-style
   mustard
2 cloves garlic, minced
¾ teaspoon dried Italian
   seasoning
¼ teaspoon coarse-grind black
   pepper

Combine all ingredients; stir until well blended.

Makes about ½ cup

Preparation Time: 5 minutes

Favorite recipe from **North Dakota Beef Commission**

BARBECUE MARINADE

½ cup chopped onion
1 tablespoon plus
    1½ teaspoons packed
    brown sugar
1 tablespoon vegetable oil
⅓ cup *each* cider vinegar and
    catsup
1 tablespoon each prepared
    horseradish and water
¼ teaspoon coarse-grind black
    pepper

Cook onion and brown sugar in oil in small saucepan over medium heat until onion is tender, about 3 minutes. Add remaining ingredients; continue cooking 3 to 4 minutes, stirring occasionally. Remove from heat; cool thoroughly before adding to beef as a marinade.

Makes about ¾ cup

Preparation Time: 10 minutes
Cooking Time: 6 to 7 minutes

Favorite recipe from **North Dakota Beef Commission**

ORIENTAL MUSTARD BARBECUE SAUCE

1 bottle (10.5 oz)
    PLOCHMAN'S® Mild
    Yellow Mustard (about
    1 cup)
½ cup barbecue sauce
¼ cup hoisin sauce
¼ cup soy sauce
¼ cup packed brown sugar
2 tablespoons sesame oil
2 tablespoons Chinese rice
    wine
1 tablespoon minced fresh
    ginger
1 clove garlic, minced

Mix together all ingredients. Use as a condiment, or brush on chicken, seafood or steak during the last 15 minutes of cooking.

Makes 2 cups

Preparation Time: 5 minutes

A.1.® Dry Spice Rub

A.1.® DRY SPICE RUB

1 tablespoon peppercorn
   melange (black, white,
   green and pink)
1 teaspoon yellow mustard
   seed
1 teaspoon whole coriander
   seed
1 tablespoon firmly packed
   light brown sugar
2 cloves garlic, minced
1 (1½- to 2-pound) beef T-bone
   or sirloin steak
3 tablespoons A.1.® BOLD
   Steak Sauce

In food processor or spice grinder, combine peppercorns, mustard seed and coriander seed; process until coarsely crushed. Stir in brown sugar and garlic. Brush both sides of steak with steak sauce; sprinkle each side with spice mixture, pressing firmly into steak.

Grill steak over medium heat for 20 to 25 minutes or to desired doneness, turning occasionally. Serve with additional steak sauce if desired.   *Makes 6 servings*

SWEET 'N SPICY ONION GLAZE

1 **envelope LIPTON® Recipe Secrets® Onion Soup Mix**
1 **jar (20 oz.) apricot preserves**
1 **cup WISH-BONE® Sweet 'n Spicy French Dressing**

In small bowl, blend all ingredients. Use as a glaze for chicken, spareribs, kabobs, hamburgers or frankfurters.

Brush on during last half of grilling, broiling or baking. Glaze can be stored covered in refrigerator up to 2 weeks.

Makes 2½ cups

NOTE: Recipe can be doubled.

Also terrific with WISH-BONE® Lite Sweet 'n Spicy French-Style, Fat Free Sweet 'n Spicy French-Style, Russian or Lite Russian Dressing.

Nutritional Information Per 2-Tablespoon Serving: Calories 120, Total Fat 5 g, Cholesterol 0 mg, Sodium 250 mg

Sweet 'N Spicy Onion Glaze

SPIRITED PEACH BARBECUE SAUCE

    8 fresh California peaches,
        cut up
    1 jar (12 ounces) roasted red
        sweet peppers
    1 large onion, coarsely
        chopped
    2 cups cider vinegar
    2 cups sugar
    2 (3-inch) cinnamon sticks
 1½ teaspoons ground cloves
    1 teaspoon ground cinnamon
    ¼ cup dark rum

Purée peaches, peppers and onion in food processor. Combine peach mixture and all remaining ingredients except rum in large saucepan. Bring to boil. Reduce heat; simmer until thickened, about 50 minutes to 1 hour. Stir in rum. Use as a glaze over ham or roasted pork.

Makes about 5 cups

Nutritional Information Per ¼-Cup Serving: Calories 111, Fat trace, Sodium 2 mg, Cholesterol 0 mg

Favorite recipe from **California Tree Fruit Agreement**

ZESTY HONEY SAUCE

    1 cup bottled chili sauce
    ½ to ¾ cup honey
    ¼ cup minced onion
    2 tablespoons dry red wine
    1 tablespoon Worcestershire
        sauce
    1 teaspoon Dijon-style mustard

Combine all ingredients in saucepan and bring to boil, stirring constantly. Reduce heat and simmer, uncovered, 5 minutes. Brush sauce on meats (ribs, chicken or beef) during last 5 minutes of cooking or use as dipping sauce.

Makes 1½ cups

Nutritional Information Per 1 Tablespoon Serving: Calories 36, Fat trace, Cholesterol 0 mg

Preparation Time: Less than 30 minutes

Favorite recipe from **National Honey Board**

Side Dish Favorites

CALYPSO GRILLED PINEAPPLE

½ cup FRENCH'S®
    Worcestershire Sauce
½ cup honey
½ cup (1 stick) butter or
    margarine

½ cup packed light brown
    sugar
½ cup dark rum
1 pineapple, cut into
    8 wedges and cored*
Vanilla ice cream

To prepare sauce, combine Worcestershire, honey, butter, sugar and rum in 3-quart saucepan. Bring to a full boil over medium-high heat, stirring often. Reduce heat to medium-low. Simmer 12 minutes or until sauce is slightly thickened, stirring often. Remove from heat; cool completely.

Brush pineapple wedges with some of the sauce. Place pineapple on oiled grid. Grill over hot coals 5 minutes or until glazed, turning and basting often with sauce. Serve pineapple with ice cream and remaining sauce. Garnish as desired. Refrigerate any leftover sauce.** *Makes 8 servings*
(1½ cups sauce)

Prep Time: 15 minutes
Cook Time: 15 minutes

You may substitute other fruits, such as halved peaches, nectarines or thick slices of mangoes, for the pineapple.

**Leftover sauce may be reheated in microwave. Microwave and stir for 30 seconds at a time.*

Calypso Grilled Pineapple

Grilled Tri-Colored Pepper Salad

GRILLED TRI-COLORED PEPPER SALAD

Fresh basil leaves
1 *each* **large red, yellow and green bell pepper, cut into halves or quarters**
⅓ **cup extra-virgin olive oil**
3 **tablespoons balsamic vinegar**
2 **cloves garlic, minced**
¼ **teaspoon salt**
¼ **teaspoon black pepper**
⅓ **cup crumbled goat cheese (about 1½ ounces)**

1. Prepare barbecue grill.

2. Layer basil leaves with largest leaf on bottom, then roll up jelly-roll style. Slice basil roll into very thin slices (enough leaves to measure ¼ cup); separate into strips. Set aside.

3. Place bell peppers, skin-side down, on grid. Grill, on covered grill, over hot coals 10 to 12 minutes or until skin is charred.

4. Place charred bell peppers in paper bag. Close bag; set aside to cool 10 to 15 minutes. Remove skins with paring knife; discard skins.

5. Place bell peppers in shallow glass serving dish. Combine oil, vinegar, garlic, salt and black pepper in small bowl; whisk until well combined. Pour over bell peppers. Let stand 30 minutes at room temperature. (Or, cover and refrigerate up to 24 hours. Bring bell peppers to room temperature before serving.)

6. Sprinkle bell peppers with cheese and basil just before serving.

Makes 4 to 6 servings

STUFFED ZUCCHINI

2 medium zucchini (about
1 pound), scrubbed
2 tablespoons olive oil
1 large ripe tomato, chopped
1 green or yellow bell pepper,
finely chopped
1 cup finely cubed boiled
ham*
½ cup minced fresh basil leaves
1 can (2.8 ounces) FRENCH'S®
French Fried Onions,
divided

**You may substitute ¼ pound
spicy sausage for the boiled ham.
Cook with pepper until sausage is
browned.*

Cut each zucchini in half
lengthwise. Using a spoon or
melon baller, scoop out pulp
leaving ¼-inch shell. Set aside
zucchini shells. Finely chop pulp.

Heat oil in large skillet over high
heat. Add zucchini pulp and
tomato; cook until liquid is
evaporated, stirring often. Add
pepper, ham and basil; cook until
pepper is tender. Stir in 1 cup
French Fried Onions. Spoon filling
into shells. Sprinkle remaining
French Fried Onions on top.

Place zucchini on vegetable
grilling rack. Place on grid. Grill
15 minutes over medium coals or
until zucchini are tender.
Makes 4 servings

Prep Time: 15 minutes
Cook Time: 25 minutes

ITALIAN VEGETABLE POCKETS

1 medium eggplant (about
¾ pound)
1 small zucchini
1 small yellow squash
4 ripe plum tomatoes
1 can (2.8 ounces) FRENCH'S®
French Fried Onions
2 tablespoons olive oil
2 tablespoons FRENCH'S®
Worcestershire Sauce
2 teaspoons Italian seasoning
2 teaspoons seasoned salt
1 teaspoon garlic powder

Cut eggplant, zucchini, squash and
tomatoes into bite-size chunks;
place in large bowl. Add French
Fried Onions. Whisk together oil,
Worcestershire and seasonings in
small bowl. Pour over vegetables.
Toss well to coat evenly. Cut six
12-inch circles of heavy-duty foil.
Spoon about 2 cups vegetables in
center of each piece of foil. Fold
foil in half over vegetables. Seal
edges securely with tight double
folds.

Place packets on grid. Cook over
hot coals 15 minutes or until
vegetables are tender, opening foil
packets carefully. Serve warm.
Makes 6 side-dish servings

Prep Time: 15 minutes
Cook Time: 15 minutes

BARBECUED CORN WITH THREE SAVORY BUTTERS

12 ears corn, unhusked
Three Savory Butters (recipes follow)

Carefully peel back husks from corn; remove silk. Bring husks up and tie securely with kitchen string. Soak corn in cold water to cover 30 minutes.

Place corn on grid. Grill over medium-high coals 25 minutes or until corn is tender, turning often. Remove string and husks. Serve with your choice of savory butter.

Makes 12 servings

Prep Time: 40 minutes
Cook Time: 25 minutes

Horseradish Butter

½ cup (1 stick) butter or margarine, softened
3 tablespoons FRENCH'S® BOLD 'N SPICY® Mustard
1 tablespoon horseradish

RedHot Chili Butter

½ cup (1 stick) butter or margarine, softened
2 tablespoons REDHOT® Cayenne Pepper Sauce
1 teaspoon chili powder
1 clove garlic, minced

Herb Butter

½ cup (1 stick) butter or margarine, softened
2 tablespoons snipped fresh chives
1 tablespoon FRENCH'S® Worcestershire Sauce
1 tablespoon minced fresh parsley
½ teaspoon dried thyme leaves
½ teaspoon salt (optional)

Place ingredients for each flavored butter in separate small bowl; beat until smooth. Serve at room temperature.

Makes about ½ cup each

KIKKO–STYLE FRENCH ROLLS

4 tablespoons butter or margarine
1 tablespoon KIKKOMAN® Teriyaki Marinade & Sauce
¼ teaspoon garlic powder
4 French rolls

Combine butter, teriyaki sauce and garlic powder in small saucepan with heatproof handle; heat on grill until butter melts. Slice each roll in half lengthwise. Place rolls, cut side down, on grill 3 to 4 inches from hot coals; cook about 2 minutes, or until golden brown. Brush butter mixture equally on each toasted roll half.

Makes 4 servings

Barbecued Corn with Three Savory Butters

GRILLED CAJUN POTATO WEDGES

3 large russet potatoes (about 2¼ pounds)
¼ cup olive oil
2 cloves garlic, minced
1 teaspoon salt
1 teaspoon paprika
½ teaspoon dried thyme leaves, crushed
½ teaspoon dried oregano leaves, crushed
¼ teaspoon black pepper
⅛ to ¼ teaspoon ground red pepper
2 cups mesquite chips

1. Prepare barbecue grill. Preheat oven to 425°F.

2. Scrub potatoes under running water with stiff vegetable brush; rinse. Dry well. (Do not peel.)

3. Cut potatoes in half lengthwise, then cut each half lengthwise into 4 wedges; place in large bowl. Add oil and garlic; toss to coat well.

4. Combine salt, paprika, thyme, oregano, black pepper and ground red pepper in small bowl. Sprinkle over potatoes; toss to coat well.

5. Place potato wedges in single layer in shallow roasting pan. (Reserve remaining oil mixture left in large bowl.) Bake 20 minutes.

Grilled Cajun Potato Wedges

6. Meanwhile, cover mesquite chips with cold water; soak 20 minutes. Drain mesquite chips; sprinkle over coals. Place potato wedges on their sides on grid. Grill, on covered grill, over medium coals 15 to 20 minutes or until potatoes are browned and fork-tender, brushing with reserved oil mixture halfway through grilling time and turning once with tongs.

Makes 4 to 6 servings

GRILLED VEGETABLES AL FRESCO

    2 large red peppers
    2 medium zucchini
    1 large eggplant

Spicy Marinade
    ⅔ cup white wine vinegar
    ½ cup soy sauce
    2 tablespoons minced ginger
    2 tablespoons olive oil
    2 tablespoons sesame oil
    2 large garlic cloves, minced
    2 teaspoons TABASCO®
       pepper sauce

• Seed red peppers; cut each pepper into quarters. Cut each zucchini lengthwise into ¼-inch-thick strips. Slice eggplant into ¼-inch-thick rounds.

• In a 13×9-inch baking dish, combine Spicy Marinade ingredients. Place vegetable pieces in mixture; toss to mix well. Cover and refrigerate vegetables at least 2 hours and up to 24 hours, turning occasionally.

• About 30 minutes before serving, preheat grill to medium heat, placing rack 5 to 6 inches above coals. Place red peppers, zucchini and eggplant slices on grill rack. Grill vegetables 4 minutes, turning once and brushing with marinade occasionally. (Or, preheat oven broiler, and broil vegetables 5 to 6 inches below broiler flame for 4 minutes on each side.)

Makes 4 servings

LEMON–BUTTER GRILLED FRUIT

    3 ripe but firm bananas,
       peeled, halved and sliced
       lengthwise
    2 fresh mangoes, peeled and
       sliced
    1 fresh pineapple, cored,
       peeled, halved and cut
       into spears
       CRISCO® Savory Seasonings
       Lemon Butter Flavor
    Sugar

• Brush fruit with oil just to coat surface.

• Sprinkle lightly with sugar.

• Grill over preheated grill or under preheated broiler 4 to 6 inches from heat source, turning once, until heated through.

• Serve hot with vanilla ice cream.

Makes 6 to 8 servings

HERBED MUSHROOM VEGETABLE MEDLEY

4 ounces button or crimini mushrooms, sliced
1 medium red or yellow bell pepper, cut into ¼-inch-wide strips
1 medium zucchini, cut crosswise into ¼-inch-thick slices
1 medium yellow squash, cut crosswise into ¼-inch-thick slices
3 tablespoons butter or margarine, melted
1 tablespoon chopped fresh thyme leaves *or* 1 teaspoon dried thyme leaves, crushed
1 tablespoon chopped fresh basil leaves *or* 1 teaspoon dried basil leaves, crushed
1 tablespoon chopped fresh chives or green onion tops
1 clove garlic, minced
¼ teaspoon salt
¼ teaspoon black pepper

1. Prepare barbecue grill.

2. Combine mushrooms, bell pepper, zucchini and squash in large bowl. Combine butter, thyme, basil, chives, garlic, salt and black pepper in small bowl. Pour over vegetable mixture; toss to coat well.

3. Transfer mixture to 20×14-inch sheet of heavy-duty foil. Wrap in foil. Place foil packet on grid. Grill packet, on covered grill, over medium coals 20 to 25 minutes or until vegetables are fork-tender. Open packet carefully to serve.

Makes 4 to 6 servings

GRILLED POLENTA

2 cups milk
2 cups water
1 cup finely ground yellow cornmeal
2 tablespoons chopped fresh basil
2 tablespoons grated Parmesan cheese
1 teaspoon TABASCO® pepper sauce
1 teaspoon salt
2 tablespoons olive oil

In medium, heavy saucepan, bring milk and water to boil on grill or stovetop. Slowly add cornmeal, stirring constantly. Cook over low heat 30 to 35 minutes, stirring constantly. Add basil, Parmesan cheese, TABASCO and salt; mix well. Pour mixture into lightly greased 10-inch round cake pan and allow to cool.

To serve, slice polenta into wedges, brush with olive oil, and grill on both sides until golden brown.

Makes 6 to 8 servings

Herbed Mushroom Vegetable Medley

GRILLED GARLIC AND VEGETABLES

8 whole heads fresh garlic*
2 artichokes, trimmed and quartered
4 ears corn, cut in half
2 carrots, cut into 1-inch chunks
2 zucchini, cut into 1-inch chunks
1 cup butter or margarine
4 teaspoons dried rosemary, crushed
½ cup sliced almonds
Salt and black pepper

The whole garlic bulb is called a head.

Prepare grill. Peel outer skin from garlic, keeping cloves intact. Cut 16 (12-inch) squares of heavy-duty foil. On double thickness of foil, place 1 whole head garlic, 1 artichoke quarter, 1 corn half and ⅛ each of carrot and zucchini chunks. Repeat to make 7 more packets. Dot each packet with 2 tablespoons butter; top with ½ teaspoon dried rosemary, and 1 tablespoon almonds. Sprinkle with salt and pepper to taste. Fold up foil, leaving space around edges and crimping all ends to make packets. Place packets on grid. Grill over hot coals 40 to 45 minutes or until vegetables are tender, turning occasionally.

Makes 8 servings

Favorite recipe from **Christopher Ranch Garlic**

BUFFALO CHILI ONIONS

½ cup REDHOT® Cayenne Pepper Sauce
½ cup (1 stick) butter or margarine, melted, or olive oil
¼ cup chili sauce
1 tablespoon chili powder
4 large sweet onions, cut into ½-inch-thick slices

Whisk together RedHot sauce, butter, chili sauce and chili powder in medium bowl until blended; brush on onion slices.

Place onions on grid. Grill over medium-high coals 10 minutes or until tender, turning and basting often with the chili mixture. Serve warm. *Makes 6 servings*

Prep Time: 10 minutes
Cook Time: 10 minutes

Tip: Onions may be prepared ahead and grilled just before serving.

Buffalo Chili Onions

GRILLED SWEET POTATO PACKETS WITH PECAN BUTTER

¼ cup chopped pecans
4 sweet potatoes (about
    8 ounces each)
1 large sweet or Spanish onion,
    thinly sliced and separated
    into rings
3 tablespoons vegetable oil
⅓ cup butter or margarine,
    softened
2 tablespoons packed light
    brown sugar
¼ teaspoon salt
¼ teaspoon ground cinnamon

1. Prepare barbecue grill.

2. Meanwhile, to toast pecans, spread in single layer on baking sheet. Bake in preheated 350°F oven 8 to 10 minutes or until golden brown, stirring frequently. Remove pecans from baking sheet; cool to room temperature. Set aside.

3. Peel sweet potatoes; slice crosswise into ¼-inch-thick slices. Alternately place potato slices and onion rings on 4 (14×12-inch) sheets of heavy-duty foil. Brush tops and sides with oil to prevent drying; wrap in foil. Place foil packets on grid.

4. Grill packets, on covered grill, over medium coals 25 to 30 minutes or until potatoes are fork-tender.

5. Meanwhile, to prepare pecan butter, combine butter, brown sugar, salt and cinnamon in small bowl; mix well. Stir in pecans. Open packets carefully; top each with dollop of pecan butter.
Makes 4 servings

GRILLED POTATOES

4 medium baking potatoes,
    diced
½ cup LIPTON® Onion Butter
    (recipe follows)
Chopped parsley

On four 18×10-inch pieces heavy-duty aluminum foil, divide potatoes equally; top each with 2 tablespoons Lipton® Onion Butter and sprinkle with parsley. Wrap foil loosely around potatoes, sealing edges airtight with double fold. Grill 30 minutes or until tender. *Makes 4 servings*

LIPTON® ONION BUTTER: Thoroughly blend 1 envelope LIPTON® Recipe Secrets® Onion Soup Mix with 1 container (8 oz.) whipped butter or soft margarine or ½ pound butter or margarine, softened. Store covered in refrigerator. Makes about 1¼ cups.

*Grilled Sweet Potato Packets
with Pecan Butter*

Acknowledgments

The publishers would like to thank the companies and organizations listed below for the use of their recipes and photographs in this publication.

Alaska Seafood Marketing Board
American Lamb Council
American Spice Trade Association
Best Foods, a Division of CPC International Inc.
California Tree Fruit Agreement
Christopher Ranch Garlic
Delmarva Poultry Industry, Inc.
The HVR Company
Kikkoman International Inc.
The Kingsford Products Company
Lawry's® Foods, Inc.
Thomas J. Lipton Co.
McIlhenny Company
Nabisco, Inc.
National Honey Board
National Cattlemen's Beef Association
National Pork Producers Council
Nestlé Food Company
North Dakota Beef Commission
Perdue® Farms
Plochman, Inc.
The Procter & Gamble Company
Ralston Foods, Inc.
Reckitt & Colman Inc.
Riceland Foods, Inc.
Sargento Foods Inc.®